National
Derek Foster a ... ng

"...try reading this new release by Derek Foster, the Wasaga Beach, Ont., business guru who himself retired by 35..." — ***Maclean's*** (May 13, 2005)

"While Warren Buffett is known as the Oracle of Omaha, investment whiz Derek Foster could be labelled the Wise Man of Wasaga Beach." — ***Toronto Sun*** *(Apr. 10, 2005)*

"The 'youngest retiree' tells how to punch out of the workplace" — ***Globe and Mail*** *(Feb. 12, 2005)*

"The result of marrying the Chilton (*The Wealthy Barber*) savings discipline with the Buffett (billionaire investor) investing philosophy has proved lucrative for Mr. Foster." — ***National Post*** *(March 31, 2001)*

"But a lengthy interview and a look at his investment statements persuaded me his book is not advice in a fictional format..." — ***Toronto Star*** *(March 10, 2005)*

"Thanks to a solid investment plan and a knack for picking the right stocks he (Derek Foster) was able to retire, mortgage free, at age 34." — ***ROBTV*** *(March 14, 2005)*

Here's How **You** Can

Using the strategy of *Canada's Youngest Retiree*

Derek Foster

FOSTER, UNDERHILL FINANCIAL PRESS

Canadian Cataloguing in Publication Data

Foster, Derek, 1970 –

Stop working, here is how you can : using the strategy of Canada's youngest retiree

0-9736960-0-1

1. Retirement income—planning. 2. Investments

3. Finance, Personal. I. Title

HG179.F669 2005 332.024'014 C2004-907201-3

Published by

Foster, Underhill Financial Press

Box 29131, 3500 Fallowfield Rd. (Unit 3)

Ottawa, ON K2J 4A0 Canada

Phone toll-free at: 1-888-686-STOP (1-888-686-7867)

Or 1-613-823-2143

www.stopworking.ca

Design/formatting/production: Heidy Lawrance Associates

Printed and bound in Canada

LEGAL DISCLAIMER

This book is intended to show you how I managed to reach retirement much earlier than the average person. I was able to stop working before my 35th birthday.

However, you must realize that I am not a professional with regard to any of the information I've provided in this book. I am merely presenting what I did to reach my goal of early retirement. I am not an expert in economic, legal, taxation, investing, realty, or any other financial or related matters. The examples I provide throughout the book are just that—examples. These are intended for illustrative purposes only. They are not an indication of what rate of return or future amount of money you might have if you followed the specific examples. They are only presented to illustrate the general concepts. Before initiating any of the strategies outlined, seek the advice of a competent professional to help you.

This book is intended as a general guide and should not be viewed as the ultimate source for financial information. Further research is needed and assistance must be sought from a qualified expert, before any action is taken by the reader. For further information, there is a recommended reading list provided at the back of this book.

For full disclosure, I must say that I (Derek Foster) own many of the securities mentioned in this book. The aim of the investing section is not to give you a list of actual securities you should buy, but to show you the type of securities you should invest in. Again, no action should be taken on your part without proper advice from a qualified professional.

Furthermore, this book might contain various errors, omissions, or mistakes of either a typographical nature or within the content itself. The reader must not rely on the accuracy of any of the information given, but should seek proper verification.

The author (Derek Foster) and the publisher (Foster, Underhill Financial Press) shall have neither liability nor responsibility to any person or other legal entity with respect to any sort of loss or damage or perceived damage caused, or alleged to have been caused by the information provided in this book. By reading this book, you fully accept these conditions. If for any reason, you do not wish to be bound by any or all of the above conditions, you may simply return this book to the publisher for a full refund.

ACKNOWLEDGEMENTS

How can I begin to thank all the individuals who offered behind the scenes support so that I could achieve my dream—to write this book? Written words can't begin to convey the deep sense of gratitude I have.

First, I would like to thank my wife, Hyeeun. Without her unwavering support and her willingness to "hold down the fort" while I wrote, this book would simply not have been possible.

To my mother, Tina Colonnese, a special thank you for your patience, ideas, and input.

To my father, William Foster, thank you for your advice and support.

To Chris Dubourdieu, my patient friend, who listened while I rambled on about whatever thought I had in mind. Your simple questions made me think more clearly.

To my dear friend John Rest, thank you for the valuable input you provided.

To Alan Dickson, who has written a couple of books, thank you for the time you spent helping me navigate the writing and publishing maze.

Finally, I would like to thank the "Three wise men,"

David Chilton, Peter Lynch, and Warren Buffett. Thank you, David for providing me with a simple foundation for investing. Peter, the insight you offer in your books was instrumental in shortening the time it took me to reach retirement. Warren, you share your knowledge selflessly and you've made it available for all to see. It was immensely helpful in allowing me to complete the investing "puzzle" and reach my financial goals.

Thank you.

TABLE OF CONTENTS

The world is full of willing people,
some willing to work,
the others willing to let them.

Robert Frost

1

IF IT'S BROKE, FIX IT!

"Our task is not to fix the blame for the past, but to fix the course for the future."
John F. Kennedy

Not another financial book! There are many books related to investing, financial planning, and retirement strategies so why do you need another one? Essentially, books may speak volumes, but money talks! This book will show you the money—the proof! It won't use ivory tower economic theories. It simply explains exactly how I retired at 34! My personal example (although an exceptional case) proves that the strategy in this book works—and it will work for you!

I have a couple of questions for you:

1. Have you ever asked your financial advisor why he is not already retired if he's so knowledgeable about investing?
2. Are your investments working well for you?

Here's a common scenario. You decided that you needed to save for retirement and invest the money in something that will return a little more than the sorry rates of interest offered on savings accounts. You put your hard-earned $50,000 or some other amount into mutual funds and waited for them to turn into the millions of dollars that you've heard about. After a number of years you have $48,000, maybe a little more or maybe less. You are underwhelmed with the results, or downright angry. Your financial plan was not supposed to turn out this way.

You call your financial advisor to ask what's happening. Where are you going to end up financially? You get the response, "Just don't even open your investment statements." (the ostrich approach), or "You're in it for the long run." Well to quote John Maynard Keynes, "In the long run, we're all dead!"

Many people believed that somehow mutual funds could protect them if the stock markets went down. This has not been the case. Financial experts simply don't have any special power to protect investors from stock market crashes.

How can you get to the promised land of early retirement—or even retire at all?

You must plan your own retirement because you are the person who cares about it the most. If you've already come to this conclusion, then you're on the right path. Think about these questions:

1. Does your financial advisor still get paid if you fail to reach your financial goals?
2. Do mutual fund managers still get paid if your mutual funds lose money for you?
3. Does your stock broker still get paid if your stocks go down?

In all cases, the answer is yes—they all get paid. But YOU don't!

How would you react if you brought your car to a service centre to get it fixed, but they never fixed it? Would you still pay them?

This book will help you take matters into your own hands and build a successful retirement. We won't look at becoming millionaires or wait for the stock market to bring us vast riches. In reality, waiting for the stock market to help you strike it rich is like prospecting during the gold rush. A lucky few became wealthy beyond their wildest dreams. The rest of the people spent their lives sifting through and moving dirt without anything to show for their efforts. A lottery ticket works as well as this approach.

The idea that you simply have to invest some money every month and then automatically become a millionaire by a certain time is overly simplistic.

For illustrative purposes, let's look at history. In October 1929, the U.S. stock market started a major crash. This descent eventually led to the market losing over 90% of its value! It took over 25 years, a whole generation, to recover.

This wasn't an isolated incident. From 1964–1981, the U.S. markets did not increase at all. That means if you had put your money into the market in 1964 and just held on (not opened your statements ever), regardless of the ups and downs, you would have received a 0% return on your money (excluding dividends) for that 17 year period!

We've all heard that things are different now, but are they? That's what was said right before the tech bubble burst in 2000 and investors lost a small fortune. As Winston Churchill said, "Those who fail to learn from history are destined to repeat it."

Is this the beginning of a 17-year stretch with zero gains? Is this the beginning of another 1929? If it is, how would it affect your retirement plans?

The stock market can be risky. You don't want to be held captive to the gyrations of the overall markets.

This book offers a different approach. It'll show you the strategy I used to retire while NOT being held captive to the financial markets. It's not a silver bullet—achieving financial independence is not an overnight project. But if you follow all the steps in the following pages, you will reach retirement safely and earlier than you thought.

The main emphasis of this book will be on investing. Then there are some tips on simplifying your spending, how to pay off your mortgage, getting out of debt and reducing the taxes you pay. The advantages and disadvantages of Registered Retirement Savings Plans (RRSPs) will also be evaluated. These steps are also an important part of reaching early retirement.

This strategy has been tested and it passed with flying colours. I started my plan for exiting the work world in 1992. I successfully retired in 2004—right after the worst bear market (stock market correction) in a generation! My retirement is intact! I'm not just talking the talk, I'm walking the walk. This is the unequivocal proof that this strategy will work for you. Unshackle yourself from both wage slavery and financial dependence on the stock market. This book will show you how.

Enjoy!

2

THE ULTIMATE PERK? 52 WEEKS ANNUAL VACATION!

Ride a wild horse, hold tight to the reins,
Adrenaline pumping all through your veins,
Your dreams—you must catch them
or they'll slip away,
Don't put off 'til tomorrow,
what can be today.
Derek Foster

I wrote the above poem, and it carries two meanings for me. First, it reminds me of one particular wonderful day I had when I was backpacking around Australia. I had signed up for a bus tour called "Oz Experience." This bus tour was unique in a number of ways. First, it was filled with other backpackers from around the world. During the bus trips you got to know one another while you exchanged stories and played numerous card games. The time and distances seemed to pass quickly on those trips. At night your new friendships were reinforced over a few beers down at the local pub.

The route the bus took was also unique in that it stopped in many "off the beaten track" places. The big destinations were a very small part of the overall experience. It was on the smaller stops where the most exciting things happened.

This brings me to the above poem. One of the stops I decided to make was in a small town called Bingara. This is a tiny little place that you'd surely miss if you blinked while driving through it. And yet it's beautiful and it will always hold a special place in my heart. I stayed there for about a week, even though I could have seen the whole town in about 5 minutes. I spent time with an Australian cowboy named John and another fellow from Ireland. We rounded up cows, broke (tamed) horses, went riding, and practiced shooting a gun. On my fourth day there, John received a new horse—a former race horse. The goal was to calm the horse down and use it for regular riding. John rode it for a while. Then I asked him if I could.

His expression told me he didn't think it was a good idea. He viewed me as a real city boy (which was pretty accurate) and didn't feel I should do it. I told him I really wanted to, so he gave me a few pointers on how to ride and let me go. I was up in the saddle and off to the races.

Wow! What an experience! The horse started to

gallop as soon as I got on. I pulled on the reins to get it to stop, but my efforts failed. We galloped down a trail and jumped over a stream. I almost fell off! I had to duck to avoid hitting a tree branch. I had never been this terrified in my life. But I held on and eventually got the horse to stop. In retrospect it was probably a stupid thing to do, but I am so happy I did it. I've ridden my wild horse!

Secondly, the above poem is also a metaphor for life. Everyone carries around dreams with them—something they absolutely want to do before they die. The sad fact is that many people die before fulfilling their dreams. Day to day life gets in the way. This is the reason to retire. It gives you the time you need to pursue your dreams, whatever those dreams might be.

When are you the happiest? Usually we're happy when we're totally engaged in an activity—one that challenges our capabilities and tests us to our limits. An example of this would be when you are playing a sport. I remember when I was a kid and I would meet my friends and we would play soccer, football, or street hockey. We were so focused on our game that we were oblivious to all other happenings around us. These were some of the happiest times of my life! Take the time to observe kids as they play. They tend to be so excited and carefree. This is the feeling that entering retirement and pursuing your dreams should be like.

Retirement gives you the freedom to enjoy your

everyday life a whole lot more. You don't have to encounter all those things that you really don't like such as rush hour traffic, your boss who always seems angry, time deadlines, office politics, or annoying alarm clocks!

The start of each day can be exciting. After I walk my children to school, I am free to pursue anything I want. I am amazed at the number of people who have said that they wouldn't know what to do with themselves if they didn't work. I truly can't understand this.

Life offers endless opportunities on a daily basis. You can read a book, talk with your spouse, play a round of golf, write a poem, try something you have never done before—or you can take some time to reflect on how lucky you are to have the life you do and be in good health and able to enjoy it.

If I ever feel bored I look at my list of "Things to do before I die." It gives me direction and allows me to think about things I would like to do while I am able to do them—my dreams. My list is always growing, always changing. But it reinforces that there is so much to do in this world.

"Things to do before I die"

- learn a musical instrument
- bungee jump
- learn to box
- paraglide

- write a book
- improve my French and Korean
- see my kids grow up
- visit all the continents
- scuba dive a wreck
- go hang gliding
- make a personal relationship with God
- make a difference somehow (volunteer)
- do the Reserves basic training
- bike across Canada
- stay at the underwater hotel I read about
- go to an annual meeting
- earn my M.A. and PhD
- learn how to design a web site
- learn to ride a motorcycle
- practice meditation
- grow my own garden
- coach football
- go to a nude beach
- climb the Sydney Harbour Bridge (they have this available)
- write a song (even if nobody wants to listen to it)
- try one night of stand up comedy

The above is just a small portion of my overall list. I know I probably won't get it all done before I die, but that's really not the point. The point is to dare to dream and then follow through. Everyone's list will be different. The lists are for ourselves and nobody else. Think of all the dreams you had when you were a child. If you search deep down, you'll find what you really want out of life. No kid ever dreamed of simply finding a nice stable job with a good pension and working there until he or she could collect it. Veer off, take a different path—retire early.

Retirement frees you up to do all those things you've always wanted to do "when you get the time." If I envision myself on my deathbed (hopefully in the distant future), I really don't think that I am going to regret not spending more time working. If I drop dead tomorrow, I feel in my heart that I have truly lived—and this feeling is extremely important to me. How about you? Do you still have some "wild horses" to ride? That's what this book will help you do.

3

MONEY ISN'T EVERYTHING, BUT...

"It is the greatest mathematical discovery of all time."

Albert Einstein—referring to compound interest

It's strange to think that the man who introduced the theory of relativity also contemplated compound interest. It was also Einstein who created the "rule of 72." This is merely a rule that states if you divide 72 by your compound rate of return, you'll figure out how long it will take for you investment to double. For example, if your rate of return is 8%, it would take you (72/8 = 9), 9 years to double your money. If you earn 12%, it would only take you (72/12 = 6), 6 years to double your money. Doubling your money a number of times is the key to achieving financial independence and proper investing is the way to do it. You need a retirement "war chest" to ensure that you not only have the time to pursue your life's passions, but also the money.

The process of investing is merely putting money aside today in the hopes of having more money in the future. There are a number of vehicles which can achieve this including bank accounts, gold, rare coins, collectibles, real estate, and stocks and related investments.

Bank Accounts

Bank accounts are a great way to store your money in the short term. In Canada you know that your money is absolutely safe with balances of less than $60,000 because these balances are protected by the Canadian Deposit Insurance Corporation (CDIC). If you have more than $60,000, you can merely get additional accounts at other Canadian financial institutions that are covered by CDIC and get an additional $60,000 of protection at each institution. In addition, Canadian banks tend to be quite stable. Deposits held at banks are also extremely liquid as you can access your money whenever you need it. The drawback of bank accounts is the fact that your money doesn't grow at a very fast rate. In fact, it is quite likely that your money won't even keep pace with inflation. In addition to this, all income earned from bank account is taxed at your top marginal rate so when you factor this into the mix, you might actually be losing ground. All in all, bank accounts should only be used for short term savings.

Gold

Gold has had an effect on mankind for thousands of years. Wars have been fought, pirates have roamed the seas, and people have died for this precious metal. During the Second World War some people in Europe sewed gold into their clothing to bribe their way to freedom. When it seems like everything is going to hell in a hand basket, the proverbial "chicken littles" of the world will tout how gold is going to be the only true store of value. This has worked on occasion in the past, but gold has too many negatives to merit your consideration as an investment. It doesn't tend to increase in value very quickly over the long term. Although it can be liquid (you can sell it easily) if bought in certificate form, you run the risk of cashing out at the wrong time and losing some of your capital (your original investment). In fact, "black gold" (oil) is a much better investment and it is also a hedge against inflation. We'll look at it a little later and show you how you can get paid to own it on a regular basis.

Rare Coins and Collectibles

Some people like to collect antiques, paintings, coins, stamps, etc. as investments. There are too many negatives to really consider this as a possible investment strategy. You have to store the items and hope that they go up in value. How does one know what will go up? What if they get damaged? I'm not saying that it's not possible, but buying and selling collectibles just seems like a lot of work. If you are an expert then go ahead, but otherwise avoid these.

Real Estate

One of the best investments around is real estate. Real estate has many advantages. First, you can use leverage (borrow money to buy it). For example, let's suppose that you have $25,000 in the bank that you decide to put to work. You can buy a $100,000 condo apartment and get a mortgage for the remaining $75,000. If you can rent it out to cover your costs, you're doing okay. You would be paying a little more of the mortgage off every month. Each month you would own a little more of the unit. If things continued to go well, eventually you'd own the whole thing and be collecting rent every month and putting it in your pocket. The disadvantages in being a landlord include getting calls in the middle of the night to go fix something, collecting the rent, or trying to find a good tenant. That's why you should focus on buying an indirect ownership (which we'll cover later) in real estate where you can benefit from the rent being collected without all the hassles. We'll look at some examples of this later on.

Bonds

There's an old saying, "Gentlemen prefer bonds." They are seen as a safer alternative to stocks. But what are bonds? Bonds are essentially IOUs issued by companies or governments. They pay a regular interest payment and run for a certain length of time (maybe 1 to 30 years). Government bonds are considered to be the safest kind if they're issued by a stable government such as Canada. Many third world countries have defaulted on their bonds, so these are not considered safe. Government bonds issued by stable countries usually pay a low rate of interests because of the safety factor. You can also buy provincial and even municipal bonds which have varying degrees of safety.

Corporate bonds are similar to government bonds, but usually pay a higher rate of interest. If a company is a solid blue chip company (stable, established company), the interest rate you get might not be much higher than government bonds. Small, unproven companies would pay a much higher rate of interest but you might never get your original investment back.

Bonds are not a great long-term investment for three reasons. First, the interest is taxed at your highest rate. The taxes are much lower for stocks. Therefore by investing in stocks you get to keep more of the money you've earned. Second, bonds have historically provided a lesser rate of return over the long-term than stocks have. So using Einstein's rule of 72, you'll be doubling your money more quickly with stocks. Finally, bonds don't offer the same amount of inflation protection. Inflation is the arch nemesis of any aspiring retiree. Every year your dollars become less and less valuable. Bonds don't guard against this like stocks do.

Some people will point to inflation protected bonds, but the rates on these are very low. Others will point to the safety of bonds, but let's see how safe they are once interest rates start rising again. As interest rates rise, the prices of bonds fall. We've been in a period of falling interest rates since 1981. Rates will start heading back up eventually, and when they do, bonds will get hammered. You can just hold onto your bonds until maturity (when you get the original investment back), but how much will this original amount be worth once inflation has taken its bite out of the value? If you want to hold a small portion in your portfolio for diversification then hold them in your RRSP (if you really want to have them) because at least you won't get hit with the high taxes you have to pay on these. However, overall you should buy shares of quality companies (we'll examine these later) that increase their dividends over time and then just sit back and collect the dividends. Bond holders never get increased payments!

Mutual Funds and the Stock Market

Well as far as investing goes, stocks are the best investment. In fact, it was investing in stocks and similar investments that allowed me to free myself from being a wage slave and to enter the world of retirement so early. Equity mutual funds would also be included in this area, but we'll look at them more closely a little later.

People have a love/hate relationship with the stock market. There are periods where everyone giggles with delight as the prices of stocks they've bought march relentlessly up—magnifying their wealth at a furious pace (think back to the late 1990's up until 2000 to remember this). Then we get a "bear" market where prices drop faster than they rose and savings evaporate faster than a puddle of water on a hot summer day. During these times many swear off investing in stocks and head for the safety of bonds or guaranteed investment certificates (GICs).

Now I don't enjoy the stomach-turning leaps and drops any more than anyone else. But the reality is that they have always existed, and always will. Think of the stock market as an elevator. It goes up and it goes down. The only difference is that with an elevator you have buttons so that you can choose which direction you want it to go.

Stock analogy: Investing in the stock market (either directly or through mutual funds) is like being in an elevator but having no buttons to control its direction!

It'll go up, then suddenly drop, then move up again. Sometimes it might drop many floors with increasing speed! You have no control! That's why I developed an investment strategy that would make my retirement plans impervious to market crashes. If you want to build up a reasonable nest egg in order to stop working and enjoy living more, the stock market is still one of the quickest paths to get you there. But you have to do it right! In the following chapters you'll see a strategy of how to invest in stocks and different kinds of investment trusts (similar to stocks) and use them to help reach your goal of early retirement without worrying about the state or direction of the stock market.

4

GETTING ANSWERS FROM "THE THREE WISE MEN"

Rules of Investing:
1. Don't lose money
2. Remember rule #1
Warren Buffett

Let me clear this up right away. I love the stock market! I love stocks! It is the stock market and the ability to buy little pieces of businesses that has allowed me to say goodbye to the rat race at such a young age! Every morning when I wake up without the alarm clock and think of how life used to be when I had to work for a living, I thank my lucky stars that I got interested and started investing in stocks at an early age. If you examine the list of the richest people in the world, you'll notice that if you ignore the people who inherited their fortunes ("lucky womb syndrome" as Warren Buffet calls it) and focus on the people who created their own fortunes, most of them have done so by owning companies.

Buying stocks is essentially buying a little piece of a business. You should think of yourself as a business owner. This can be really powerful. For example, look at Wal-Mart. At this company many of the workers make minimum wage. They can also take part in a company stock purchase plan. There are some minimum wage employees who have become millionaires simply by buying little pieces of Wal-Mart over time. They are much wealthier than many of the people they knew who had much "better" jobs with higher salaries. I've never seen anyone on the list of the richest people who got there by working at a job and getting promotions and raises. Ownership is where it's at!

Having said all that, the stock market is not an expressway to financial freedom. It's more of a meandering road. It takes time, diligence, and patience. It's not easy. But if you stay the course and follow the path, the rewards can be enormous.

My first introduction to the stock market was when I was 14 years old. I had decided what I wanted to be when I grew up—rich! I wanted to play football in the NFL (National Football League). But just in case that didn't work out, I decided I wanted to learn about the stock market. I remember my mom decided to buy me a book to nurture my interest. I believe the book was called, *How to Buy Stocks*. It explained why companies sold shares to the public and how to buy them. It was interesting, but after reading it, I went on dreaming about how I was going to become a famous running back in either the NFL or CFL.

Five years later, I was in my first year of university. I needed a summer job to help pay the bills and landed a job at Radio Shack. It was a reasonable summer job, but I was really excited by the fact that as an employee I could contribute a portion of my pay into a stock purchase plan that the company had arranged. This allowed employees to buy shares of the company on favourable terms. I was young and impatient and I decided that although the share plan was good, I would invest my entire life savings into Intertan (which owned Radio Shack in Canada). I knew nothing about the company and had never read the annual report. However, I opened a brokerage account and deposited my life savings of around $5,000 and bought shares of Intertan.

Well as the saying goes, "A fool and his money are soon parted." (I was the fool!). I thought I had bought the shares at such a good price. They had been selling for over $60 a share at one point, but I had bought them for only $24 each—a sixty percent discount! What a deal! Well, I had no idea why the shares had fallen (and still don't), but they fell further, down to $20, $18, then $15. I was riding the stock market "elevator," but it was moving the wrong way and I had no buttons to press! A year or two later I saved up a little more money and bought more shares. If they were a great deal at $24, then they must be a steal at $15! Or so I thought. The share price remained constant for a while and then fell a bit more to $12 each. I felt sick to my stomach every day and finally decided to sell them. I had lost a few thousand dollars (and a few pounds), but I had learned an important lesson.

Investing Rule #1: Don't ever buy stocks—they're too risky!

But I started this chapter saying how much I love stocks. I eventually went back to investing in stocks directly but I had learned a valuable lesson. First, you must figure out what you are doing before investing in anything. You must research every investment thoroughly. Get some books about investing and learn what you're doing. At the back of this book, there is a list of books you might want to read before investing. Now I've had people tell me that reading investment books is too hard. Well it may be hard, but it's a lot easier than getting up and going to work day after day for 20 or 30 years longer than you have to just because that's the only way you know how to make money. Investing (with the proper knowledge) brings financial freedom. Over time, this original rule changed to:

*Investing Rule #1(amended): Don't ever buy stocks—
they're too risky—if you
don't understand them.*

It would be a few more years before I waded back into the market without someone holding my hand. In the meantime, I had landed a summer job at MD Management, which is an investment arm for the Canadian Medical Association. I was an accounting student and was spending time doing a special project. However, what really interested me was all the talk amongst my experienced coworkers about investing and mutual funds. Then my supervisor handed me a book on investing. This was my introduction to the thinking of the first wise man, David Chilton. The book was a best seller called, *The Wealthy Barber.* It was then and there, at age 22, that I decided to start investing seriously and try to retire as early as possible.

Mutual funds seemed like such a wonderful vehicle for wealth accumulation. They didn't seem to require an incredible amount of knowledge. You simply signed up for a regular investment program and contributed monthly to a huge fund. This fund would collect money from thousands of other investors. Through this fund you could have a professional manager make decisions about where to put your money. This seemed like the perfect route to take. After having been so rudely jolted into reality with my first foray into the market, mutual funds seemed like a safer way to invest. Sort of like when teenagers are learning to drive, but they don't quite have the hang of it yet. They will get a learner's permit and be able to drive only when an experienced driver is right there beside them. This ensures they don't "crash"—invest in something stupid and lose their money (like my brilliant example explained above).

Investing *Rule #2: If you don't feel you can invest on your own, buy mutual funds.*

Over the next few years I religiously put away $200 every month into my pre-selected mutual funds. Together these funds increased nicely. In the meantime I was reading just about anything I could get my hands on related to investing. I made daily visits to the university library to read the Financial Post (now part of the National Post), The Globe and Mail, and the business section of the local paper. I stopped by the bookstore whenever I could and looked for various books on investing. It was around this time that I discovered a few important facts that would shorten my road to retirement.

The first thing I began to realize was that although investing in mutual funds was a great way to get the benefits of a rising stock market, there was indeed a cost. These funds charged management fees ranging from a little over 1% to well over 2.5% per year. To illustrate the importance of this finding, look at the following calculations. In the first example, the underlying stocks earn 12% a year if you buy them directly on your own. In the second example, if you have to pay a mutual fund manager a 2% annual management fee to manage your investments, the rate of return is reduced to 10% (12%-2%). In both examples, we'll assume $50,000 is invested for 30 years.

1. $50,000 invested @ 12% for 30 years gives you approximately	$1,498,000
2. $50,000 invested @ 10% for 30 years gives you approximately	$ 872,000
Total difference (1,498,000–872,000)	**$ 626,000**

As you can see, the management fees can really add up over time. The difference between investing by yourself and paying the 2% management fee works out to over half a million dollars! That's a huge price to pay to have "someone sit beside you while you drive." The only time you should buy mutual funds is when you are starting out at investing and don't have a large enough nest egg to achieve diversification. They're a good vehicle for regular monthly investments but once you have $20,000 or more, start buying stocks directly!

The only other reason you might invest in mutual funds is if you don't know how to buy stocks correctly (refer to my stunning example at the beginning of the chapter). Just remember that if you choose the mutual fund route, it'll cost you a lot of money (see the example above). Knowing how to properly buy the correct stocks will be the main focus of the rest of this book.

One final point to remember is that if your mutual funds make money for you, the mutual fund manager also makes a lot of money. If your mutual funds lose money for you, the mutual fund manager *still* makes money. You risk your own money but only reap some of the potential rewards.

Investing Rule #3: If you learn how to invest on your own, buy stocks directly to improve returns.

It was right then that I decided that if I wanted to retire as early as possible, I would have to learn how to invest on my own. If I could match the rate of return of the mutual fund managers, I could save the 2% management expenses and my retirement fund would grow much faster. However this seemed like such an ambitious goal. How could I perform as well as the professional mutual fund managers? How could I match their results without the huge research department they had at their disposal? I stumbled upon the answer to my dilemma. The answer was contained in an investing book entitled, *One up on Wall Street.*

One up on Wall Street was a book written by Peter Lynch, the second wise man in my journey to financial freedom. He is a well-respected investor and an American mutual fund manager who worked for Fidelity Investments, which is one of the biggest mutual fund companies in the US. Peter's track record of investing while he managed the Magellan fund, Fidelity's largest fund, was incredible. If you want valuable insight into investing I would strongly recommend this book along with the book he published shortly afterwards entitled, *Beating the Street.* In both these books Peter reveals how he goes about finding great investments and showing what exactly a great investment is. One of the books started off by describing how an elementary school class learned how to choose investments that outperformed the majority of mutual fund managers in the US. It was upon reading this that I decided that I too could manage my own investments and thus shorten my journey to retirement.

One of the stock investing secrets that was revealed to me while reading was only covered quickly. Peter mentions that one method for choosing stocks is only to invest in companies that made it onto the *High Dividend Achievers* list. A dividend is merely a cash payment the company makes to all its owners (shareholders). However, it was this piece of advice that formed one of the cornerstones of my investment philosophy. A company that has the ability to raise its dividend every year becomes a very valuable investment over time. The companies on the high dividend list have managed to raise their dividends consecutively for many years. You can look for these companies on *Mergent's List of High Dividend Achievers*.

The second fact that has stuck in my mind and become part of my investing strategy was also mentioned by Peter. Simply don't invest in a company that a little kid can't understand. In other words, keep it simple! You don't need to invest in complex companies to reap outsized profits. In fact, the reverse is usually true. Focus on investing in stocks of companies you know and understand and over time you'll do well.

My investment approach evolved gradually but reading these two books gave me the beginnings of an investment foundation. At around the same time, another major piece of my investment approach was being formulated. I was beginning to read everything I could get my hands on about Warren Buffett.

Warren Buffett is to investing what Wayne Gretzky, Mario Lemieux, and Bobby Orr all rolled into one would be to hockey. He is the third and perhaps most influential of the wise men who led me on my journey. He is by far the most successful investor of all time.

During the nineties he was playing leap frog with Bill Gates for the position as richest person in America. At last count, Warren had wealth amounting to over $40 billion. Most of that wealth is concentrated in his company, Berkshire Hathaway.

Berkshire is a unique company in many respects. First, you need to spend almost $100,000 U.S. to buy 1 share of the company. There are "B" shares (one thirtieth of a regular share) which trade at around $3,000 each. The company does not pay any dividends even though it is sitting on billions of dollars in cash! Over the years, Buffett has invested in a range of businesses including a candy shop, Dairy Queen, a shoe maker, a furniture store, Benjamin Moore paints, and many others. He's also owned stock in Gillette, Coca Cola, Washington Post, American Express, and many others. The main focus of the company is insurance. If you ever want to study investing, you have to read whatever Buffett has to say. The easiest way is to type Berkshire Hathaway into the internet and read all his chairman letters from previous annual reports. This collection is a gold mine of information on investing.

From Buffett I've incorporated a few fundamental ideas. First, everyone has an area in which they're familiar with and you should only invest in these areas. This is another way of saying to only invest in what you know and understand. Warren has made his billions investing in things like soft drinks rather than computer chips or other things he simply does not understand well enough. If you want to be successful at investing, stick with companies you understand.

The second piece of information that Warren gives comes from his mentor, Benjamin Graham (who was a very wise man himself). Graham is considered to be the father of fundamental analysis, as he was the first person to study value and create a framework by which one could value a business. If you ever want to learn more about Graham's investment philosophy, pick up a copy of, *The Intelligent Investor*. Buffett studied under Graham and a lot of his ideas originally came from Graham.

Anyone who has ever followed the stock market over time will notice that it seems to go up and down rather quickly and randomly. There often doesn't seem to be any rhyme or reason for this (the "elevator without buttons"). One piece of economic news could send the markets down and then another development can send them up just as quickly. In *The Intelligent Investor*, Graham argued that the stock market was irrational in the short term and created an analogy that can be very useful in times of market turmoil. This piece of advice is to view the stock market as a manic depressive individual. Sometimes he is extremely optimistic and quotes you a ridiculously high price and other times he is depressed and is willing to buy or sell stocks at fire sale prices. I think of this analogy whenever everyone seems to be saying that the sky is falling. Simply ignore the short term swings. When all the headlines are saying that the world is coming to an end, this is the time to be brave, step up, and buy.

It was a combination of David Chilton laying down the basic foundation, followed by the ideas from Peter Lynch and Warren Buffett (who got some ideas from Graham), that helped me devise my investing strategy and led to my being in a position to retire at the age of 34.

We are told that we can't possibly perform as good as the "investment professionals," so you should just hand them your money to invest for you. I bought into this whole line of thinking early on, but my strategy changed over time. It's true that the foundation to building a comfortable retirement lies in "paying yourself first" and investing the difference in some way. This advice is commonplace. The problem is that many of the "professionals" have dismal track records. They don't have a special crystal ball which tells them what to buy. Most mutual funds fail to keep up with the market! Think about it. If the "professionals" are so smart at investing, why aren't they retired too? Why aren't they on the list of richest people competing with the likes of Warren Buffet as richest investor? Don't buy into the idea that stock brokers or mutual fund managers have some special power to predict the stock market and make you rich. Have these people succeeded in making you rich so far?

How should you invest then? I would advise the same strategy I used—it's worked for me. Simply open a discount brokerage account. You can transfer your current holdings there—even your mutual funds. Then build a strong, crash-proof portfolio gradually—brick by brick. Get rid of weak companies and buy good solid companies gradually as they go on sale. You can see the criteria to look for as well as some examples in the following chapters.

5

LET'S PRAY FOR A STOCK MARKET CRASH!

"Do you know the only thing
that gives me pleasure?
It's to see my dividends come in"
John D. Rockefeller

My investment philosophy evolved over a number of years. I learned a lot from reading about investing and even more through trial and error. In the end, I created a basic list of things to look for. A lot of these ideas mirror the concepts that have been presented by many other investors over time. Once you find something that works you stick with it. The ideas below are mostly from Warren Buffett (billionaire investor) and Peter Lynch (former fund manager), blended together with some of my own ideas. Here are my basic investing tenets:

1. Only invest in companies you understand
2. Only invest in companies that pay a dividend (preferably a rising dividend)
3. Look for companies that are selling cheaply (the old adage of buy low, sell high)
4. Invest in companies that are "recession-proof"
5. Don't focus on foreign companies
6. Only invest in companies that are dominant in their industry (or that cannot be seriously hurt by a larger competitor)
7. Only invest in companies that have displayed a long history of strong performance
8. Only invest in companies that have a strong brand loyalty among its customers
9. Once you've bought the perfect company, never sell it!

These tenets formed the basis of my investment philosophy. As I mentioned earlier, my philosophy evolved over time, but whenever I lost on an investment, it seems like one of the above tenets had been broken. Following them increased my investment success and allowed me to retire at 34. Let's take a closer look at each one of them.

Investing Tenet #1: Invest only in companies you understand.

Right off let me say that I have never bought a technology stock. I am someone who does not own a cell phone, fax machine, flat screen TV, or even the latest computer. It is a sad fact but I am living a simple existence like people did in the 1950's. I don't get excited about new inventions unless I can see a clear benefit to my life. For example, a cell phone seems like a nuisance. Why would I want to be available 24 hours a day? I like to disconnect from the world for a while every day and be totally on my own. I usually keep a little money on me so if I urgently need to make a phone call I can just plunk a quarter into the nearest pay phone and dial.

In spite of my disinterest in technology in general, I am not a technophobe. I love the internet and really can't figure out how I lived before it came along. It's such a powerful resource. But I am petrified about investing in technology companies. Simply put, I'm not smart enough to understand these sorts of companies, but smart enough to avoid investing in them.

Focus on things like supermarkets, consumer product companies, utility companies, etc. Companies whose products or services you use every day. They're easy to understand. But trying to figure out which technology is going to be dominant in the future or more precisely, which firm will dominate this new technology is beyond most of us.

Now you might point to a company like Microsoft and point out that Bill Gates is the world's richest man and that he got there by dealing with technology. This is true, but how do you determine what the next Microsoft will be? It's too risky, so I don't play that game. Remember, "not losing money" is the first step to successful investing.

Investment Tenet #2: Only invest in companies that pay a dividend.

This is a rule that I created and I follow it religiously. A company must pay you a dividend (send you a cheque) every year. This rule will prohibit you from buying many companies that have turned out to be wonderful investments, but it also helps you avoid major pitfalls as well. Remember Warren Buffett's rule #1 (Don't lose money). If you can find a company that pays a dividend and has a history of increasing that dividend over time, without any dividend cuts (reductions in the money it pays you), then you've found yourself a solid investment. This preference is rooted in the phrase, "A bird in the hand...." This tenet is so fundamental to investment success that the entire next chapter expands on it. This is the factor that will allow your retirement portfolio to survive stock market crashes. Once you've bought an investment that pays a steady stream of dividends that increase over time, you should have no interest in selling it...ever! It doesn't matter if the stock market crashes, as the cash will still flow to you on a regular basis. If there's a stock market crash, simply buy more shares.

Investment Tenet #3: Buy companies that are selling cheaply.

You've probably heard the expression, "Buy low, sell high." This is a very commonly used phrase to guide investors, but it is only a partial truth. You should not seek out cheap investments first. It is far more important to seek out quality investments and then wait for something to happen that causes them to become temporarily cheap. Have you ever known anyone who buys something just because it's a "bargain"? Perhaps it's a cheap shirt, DVD player, or whatever. They are so caught up in the price that they don't think about their purchase carefully. Then a few days later, they realize that they've bought a piece of junk, but they're stuck with it. It was a dumb purchase. It's the same with investing. Focus on the quality first (companies meeting the criteria listed at the beginning of this chapter) and *then* look at the price. Develop a list of quality companies you would like to buy if the price is right. There's a strategy for finding some quality companies outlined later in this book. Then check the stock market from time to time. On occasion, when the stock market "elevator" is in a freefall (a market crash), these quality companies will go "on sale." It is then that you buy them. That's why as farmers pray for rain, you should be praying for a market crash. But only buy quality. And don't worry about "selling high." Once you've bought your quality company that pays ever increasing dividends, you're much better off to just sit back and collect the dividends forever.

Investing Tenet #4: Invest in companies that are "recession-proof."

What does this mean? You should focus on companies that aren't dependent on the general economy to do well. Let me give you a scenario. Suppose you are married and both you and your spouse earn the same amount of money. Things are comfortable. Then suddenly you find out that one of you has been laid off. You are now forced to live on half the income. How would you manage this? First, you would cut the non-essentials. For example, you might eat at home rather than dining out. You might postpone that new car purchase. Forget about the vacation. Ditch the plan to buy that new home entertainment unit. Any company that does businesses related to these types of activities is not "recession proof." Forget about buying shares in car companies, airlines, hotels, electronics retailers, etc. It does not mean that these areas cannot make great investments, sometimes they can. But remember, making sure you don't lose money is often as important as making money.

What sort of companies would be recession-proof? Supermarkets (people always have to eat), utilities (you need it regardless of the economy), banks (you still pay your mortgage), tobacco (cigarettes come before food for some people), prescription drugs (very important for health). Get the idea? Remember, just because a company operates in this area, does not automatically make it a good investment. It must meet the other criteria in this list of investing tenets to be considered a good investment.

Investing Tenet #5: Don't focus on foreign companies.

Often when you look at business magazines they tout the advantages of investing abroad. Lately, many of the articles seem to focus on an emerging China. China is one of the fastest growing economies in the world with over 1.2 billion people. Many expect that just as the U.S. overtook Great Britain to become the preeminent world power, the same destiny awaits China. Perhaps this is true, but it doesn't mean you should invest there. High tech was touted as the fastest growing sector of the economy in the late 1990's, but ask anyone who invested in any of the dot-coms (internet companies) if this fact created fabulous wealth for them. Sure there were a few winners who got in early and became millionaires in a relatively short period of time. There are also some people who chose the correct numbers in the Lotto 6/49 and they're quite well-off now, but I wouldn't recommend this as a retirement strategy. There were simply many more losers in the high tech arena than winners. Many people suffered such great financial carnage that they're not sure if they'll ever retire. The odds are against you if you try to strike it rich. The risks are simply too great.

Stay mostly right here in Canada and if you want to venture out a little, look to the U.S. There are many large companies that can give you exposure to foreign markets without having to take on all the added risks. There are many wonderful companies here in Canada which have done very well for their shareholders. Why would you want to invest in a company that you don't know anything about when you can invest in companies you use every day? Invest in what you know; stick close to home and you'll do fine.

Investing Tenet #6: Only invest in dominant companies

The story of David and Goliath is a great one. Generally people have a strong tendency to cheer for the underdog. We don't like the idea of the "little guy" being threatened or coerced by the "big bully." In business however, it is usually the biggest companies that succeed. If you're going to plunge and invest your own hard earned money, invest it with the biggest fish in the pond. Little fish tend to be eaten.

Investing Tenet #7: Invest in companies with a strong performance history.

To reduce risk, focus on companies that have a long operating history. For example, Coca Cola is one of the greatest investments of all time. I've never owned shares of it, because they've always been too expensive, but if they ever went "on sale," you should scoop some up. Coke was started in 1886 in Atlanta, Georgia and has grown to become the world's most recognizable brand. I've traveled to many countries in the world, and Coke has been sold in all of them. It has a dividend history going back to 1920 of paying uninterrupted dividends to shareholders and over 40 consecutive years of dividend increases. It's survived two world wars, the great depression, the cold war, numerous recessions, the cola wars, ...and still it continues to bring in billions of dollars as well as increased sales every year. This is the type of company you should have if it's ever priced right. There are many others like it. Focus on these long term winners.

Investing Tenet #8: Invest in companies that have a strong brand loyalty

This tenet is very important. Twenty-five years ago you could have merely walked down any supermarket aisle and looked at the various products you used regularly and bought stock in those companies. They were great. But then something happened. Gradually stores began stocking their own store brands. These store brands didn't have the expensive advertising campaigns behind them, so they were priced much cheaper. This resulted in some previously great companies losing their pricing power. For example, whenever I go shopping, if I'm looking for brown sugar, I buy the cheapest bag I can find. I'm not loyal to a certain brand. So this business has weak consumer brand loyalty, so the stocks in this area would be weaker—they compete based on price. An example of a product that carries strong brand loyalty would be children's Tylenol. When people walk into a store to buy it, they don't just ask for any brand but they request it specifically. While I was living in Korea, my son had a fever and I went to the pharmacy to get some Tylenol. They had some other brand that I had never heard of (at half the price), but which one do you think I bought? The same loyalty just doesn't exist for certain products. This fact is extremely important.

Investing Tenet #9: Once you've bought a great company, never sell!

This rule is so important. It goes against the conventional wisdom of trying to buy low and sell high. When searching for investment information you'll come across endless advice telling you to buy this or sell that. If you were to follow all of this advice, you'd be broke really quickly. The commissions and capital gains taxes would take away all the money you had earned. The media is still a good source of information, but be very slow to pull the trigger when deciding to buy stocks. The old saying, "hurry up and wait" is a good one for investing.

There's an expression that states, "if you put twelve economists in a room you'd end up with thirteen different opinions." Don't listen to economic forecasts or try to act on them.

Through life in general, the more active you are in doing something, the better the result. Investing doesn't work that way. Remember all the day traders you heard about a few years ago. They're all broke now and back at their day jobs. The most successful investor of all time (Warren Buffett) doesn't try to buy and sell quickly.

You have to be committed to the stocks you buy. It's like a marriage—"till death do us part" situation.

The "dating" came earlier when you were researching the company. That part is over now. Remember selling stocks, like divorce, comes at a high cost.

This is a basic overview of my investing foundation in a nutshell. If you follow the above guidelines, you'll avoid some of the major pitfalls that exist for many investors and ***ensure that your retirement plans never get derailed because of a stock market crash.***

6

"SHOW ME THE MONEY!" INVESTING

"Show me the money!"

From the movie *Jerry Maguire*

The above quote has become quite famous. It's synonymous with the movie *Jerry Maguire*. In the movie, Jerry, who is a sports agent, is leaving his firm and his client is telling him he will keep Jerry as his agent if Jerry can "show him the money." Now I'm not recommending you look to movies for investment advice but in this case it is quite fitting. Whenever you buy an investment, you should be expecting the investment to "show you the money." I know I listed dividends in the previous chapter, but I would like to re-emphasize them again. The faster you can get your money back in the form of dividends or distributions (cash from unit trusts, which we'll cover later), the faster you get to retire. It's that simple.

The investment industry likes to focus on determining a certain fixed sum that you should save up for retirement—perhaps $1 or $2 million. If you save (x amount) at (y %) for a certain number of years, you'll be able to retire. But you have to ask, "What if the stock market goes down?" Many will say that you just keep on investing and that eventually the markets always recover. I don't buy that! That strategy might work, but it might not! The U.S. markets didn't go up from 1964–1981—that's 17 years of no increase! It could happen again.

You know about the great crash of 1929. Here the stock markets lost approximately 90% of their value and took 25 years to recover! How would your retirement plans be affected if you portfolio lost 90%? Could you wait 25 years for it to recover? Do you want to wait 25 more years to retire? With my retirement plan, even if the stock market crashed 90%, I'd stay retired. My lifestyle wouldn't be affected. I wouldn't jump out the nearest window. Let me explain.

My strategy is different. When you buy investments, you shouldn't look for the price of your shares to increase and try to sell them for a profit. Forget "Buy low, sell high."

To illustrate the difference between my strategy and the one usually espoused by the investment industry, let me give you an analogy. Suppose you had a piece of land and that was the only thing you owned. It was your only asset. Now suppose you were trying to figure out how to use this land to create an income that would take care of you for the duration of your retirement. So you contact "Mr. Investment Representative." He advises you to plant many trees (stocks or mutual funds). Over the years they would grow, becoming quite valuable for either building materials or firewood. When you're ready to retire, all you'd have to do is cut some down every year and sell them (gradually selling your stocks). There might be years when there are fires or storms that kill some of the trees (market corrections), but over the long term you would be assured of having a very valuable asset and you take a percentage of this every year. But what if there are a number of years where the trees don't grow at all (a long period like 1964–1981 where the stock markets did not rise at all in total)? You'd be continually cutting down some of the trees without any growth replacing them. Eventually they might all be gone before they start growing again (your money is gone before the markets recover). This is the weakness of this strategy.

Now look at a different strategy. Plant trees but don't *ever* think about cutting them down! Instead of a plan for the eventual harvest, plant trees that yield fruit. Every year, the trees would grow and grow, but every year you could harvest the fruit. As sure as the sun rises daily and the seasons change yearly, your trees would bear fruit. You would sell the fruit and then you could either spend that money or reinvest it in your trees by buying more fertilizer which would help your trees grow faster and yield even more fruit the next year (buying more dividend paying stocks). In this example, the fruit represents the dividends that stocks provide. Even if you encountered many years of no growth (like the stock markets from 1964-1981), your fruit would still be reliably coming to you. This strategy is much less risky.

This is the fundamental concept of my investing theory. Only buy investments that yield fruit, or pay dividends. And only buy investments that are safe and whose dividends go up over time. These sorts of investments were covered in the last chapter and some examples of them are provided in the next chapter. With these types of investments, even if the market crashes you keep collecting cash regularly. And you NEVER sell them!

This is what's called "show me the money" investing. If you focus on companies that have a long history of paying dividends, you tend to avoid the big blowups. It's not a get rich quick idea, but it's a safe and steady path to early retirement. Here's why it's safer than only looking for stock price appreciation.

There are numerous ways in which companies can

improve the "appearance" of how well they're doing. Just look at some past examples of accounting trickery which gave the illusion that companies were earning a lot of profit, when in fact they were not! In reality, business might be terrible, but they could report ever increasing earnings or sales by "massaging the numbers." But over time, the cash doesn't lie. If a company is doing poorly, it will eventually be forced to cut or even eliminate its dividend. The reality is that companies cannot create real cash out of thin air! So companies that pay steady and rising dividends over time must have sound underlying fundamentals to support the dividend payments. Remember talk is cheap. Don't believe everything you hear about a company's prospects. Always be skeptical. Zero in on the cash that it's returning to its shareholders. That's the real story.

You will also benefit by seeing the increased cash flow coming into your account, and increasing over time. Simply stated, once the money being paid to you in dividends equals the annual income you feel you need, you can retire and never work for money again. It also soothes you during the bear markets (stock market crashes) because you see that although stock prices have fallen, your dividends are still being paid uninterrupted.

The performance of the stock market does not affect the dividends companies pay!

I've listed some companies in the following chapters that have a habit of regularly increasing their dividends regardless of how the stock market or economy is performing. The reality is that if you buy recession-proof, steady dividend paying companies, a stock market crash will not alter their dividend paying policies. The cash keeps flowing to you.

The final beauty of looking for the "fruit" in the form of dividends is that it forces you to think about buying low. For example suppose you are looking at "Big Money Company" and it seems like a good investment. Its stock is trading at $100 per share and it pays a dividend of $3. That's a 3% rate of return. You research the stock and find that it is in the habit of increasing it's dividend over time so you feel this is a great investment. The only trouble is that the stock price seems a little too expensive. So you wait.

A few months later, something happens which causes the stock markets to go down. This could be some economic event, a war, or a host of other reasons. You see the stock market is in a freefall once again. You notice all the "chicken littles" of the world talking about how everything is going to hell in a hand basket! The sky is falling! People are selling stocks indiscriminately. They are fixated on all the gloom and bailing out while they can. You check up "Big Money Company," which of course follows your investment criteria of a "recession-proof stock." Since it has a habit of raising its dividend over time, you notice that the dividend has increased and it now pays $3.30 per share. The price on the other hand has dropped by half—a 50% drop in price. That means the company's share price has fallen from $100 to $50. So it's now paying a dividend of $3.30 a share, and each share costs $50. That's a yield of 6.6% ($3.30 divided by $50)! You pick up the phone or log onto the internet and breathe deeply. You are very nervous buying while everyone else is selling. This is the hardest thing to do, but you know that sheep get slaughtered so you make the order. You take the road less traveled and buy while everyone else seems to be galloping down the path that says "sell." You step up to the plate and take a swing and buy stock of "Big Money Company." You hope you did the right thing.

As time goes on you see that the shares of "Big Money Company" have fallen another $10 and now trade at $40 a share. You've lost $10 a share or 20% of your investment. This should not matter to you though. The underlying fundamentals of the company are sound and you realize the company now pays a dividend of $3.30 a share and each share costs $40. This dividend now represents a payout of over 8% ($3.30 divided by $40)! If you have *any* money to invest you buy more shares of the company. Even if the stock price stays at $40 forever, you will get a $3.30 for each share you own...forever! In fact, if you've chosen the right company which increases its dividends regularly, you will get more money over time. So you sit there and collect your dividend cheques every three months. You basically don't care about the stock price. ***You have bought a cash flow, not a stock.*** You'll be harvesting the fruit for years to come—in ever increasing quantities.

Eventually the ominous, black clouds surrounding the markets lift and the share price of "Big Money" rebounds to $100. You've doubled your money. But you don't sell it. You don't choose to cut down the trees and sell them for firewood. You keep harvesting the fruit, year in and year out, knowing that you are that much closer to your goal of not working for money, but having your money work for you. That is the essence of "show me the money" investing. Now let's look at what investments you can buy to achieve this.

7

WHAT SHOULD YOU BUY?

"If all economists were laid end to end, they would not reach a conclusion."

George Bernard Shaw

The above quote is fitting for the foundation of stock market investing. If you read financial information, you'll see countless headlines predicting how the economy is going to perform and explaining which stocks should benefit from whatever scenario the forecaster envisions. A good rule of thumb is that if someone is giving you short-term predictions, ignore it. You will have the same results by going to your local fortune teller. Nobody can predict short-term trends.

Over the long term, the surest way to invest (and hence the quickest road to financial independence) is to buy quality, recession-proof companies that raise their dividends consistently over time. Wait patiently until the market decides to let you buy them at a bargain price. Once you've bought, simply hold them forever.

Just concentrate on spending the dividend cheques that come in every three months.

This is the best method, but acting upon it can be challenging. The first thing you must understand is that over 90% of businesses are not worth buying at any price. The universe of stocks is essentially divided into three main types—the good, the bad, and the ugly. You want good stocks (which are shown below). Avoid the bad stocks (not recession proof, weak brand loyalty, etc.) and especially avoid the ugly (companies that have no real earnings or imaginary earnings). The ugly stocks rose to prominence during the tech bubble!

This begs the question, "Why are some investors so focused on diversifying and index funds (mutual funds that invest in every company in an index) when most investments are not worth owning?" Most companies are simply not good enough to warrant your attention. They may seem cheap, but they're cheap for a reason. So the most difficult part is finding the true winners.

Focusing on Canadian stocks is advisable for a number of reasons. I know many people will point to the superior returns investors have reaped from American stock markets over time, but a large portion of the gain has been from the long-term depreciation of the Canadian dollar. Now I'm not saying I'm an economist and I have no clue what the Canadian dollar will be trading at many years from now, but there are no guarantees that it will continue to fall vis-à-vis the greenback. Canadian governments have gotten their collective financial houses in order while the U.S. has not, so you might even see a gradual rise in the value of the Canadian dollar. In fact the Canadian dollar was worth more than a U.S. dollar as recently as the 1970's. Regardless, if you are going to be retiring in Canada and spending most of your money in Canada, it makes financial sense to keep most of your assets in Canada.

The other important reason to buy Canadian stocks is the fact that the dividend income is taxed much more favourably than with American stocks. With U.S. stocks you must pay a 15% withholding tax up front. Then the remaining portion of your dividend is taxed at your top tax rate! Canadian dividends benefit from the Dividend Tax Credit which we'll review in the tax chapter of this book. This means that you pay your taxes, but also get a tax credit that reduces the total amount of taxes you end up paying. You can research it further if you are interested, but the important thing to remember is that dividends from Canadian companies receive favourable tax treatment.

Others will tout the advantage of diversifying globally. Canada represents approximately 3% of the total world markets, so you are limiting yourself if you only invest in Canada, or so the line of thinking goes. But how can you trust the foreign accounting? Are you familiar with these foreign companies? In addition, the costs of investing in these foreign companies are much higher.

You also usually pay a higher rate of tax on the dividends you receive. You should have some diversification, but don't overdo it. The U.S. stock market provides ample opportunities to augment your Canadian holdings. Going beyond this has been unnecessary for me.

The trouble arises because economically speaking, Canada is so small. The economy is only 10% the size of the American one. This creates fewer Canadian stocks that meet the criteria of sound investments. This problem is compounded by the fact that Canada tends to gain so much of it's wealth through natural resources (mining, forestry, etc.). And quite frankly natural resource companies are not where you should invest your money (in most cases) because they lack many of the criteria of a good company (not recession-proof, inconsistent dividends, etc.). Their fortunes tend to rise and fall with the general economy and there are not too many steady performers in this area. Having mentioned this, there are some wonderful Canadian companies that would make great investments. Below I've listed a few possibilities.

The Big Canadian Banks

Few people switch banks once they've established a relationship with one. The fact is that the inconvenience of changing accounts from one bank to another keeps customers where they are. The banks earn money from a wide range of products including mutual funds, mortgages, insurance, brokerage fees, credit cards, etc. You name it! The big banks have been around for a number of years and profits continue to climb along with their dividends. Barring some cataclysmic event, if you buy shares in any one of them you should have an investment that pays you a secure, ever increasing quarterly dividend.

Let's take a quick look at RBC Financial (Royal Bank). This bank was originally founded in 1864 so it pre-dates Confederation. It was originally called the Merchants" Bank but later changed its name to Royal Bank. It employs thousands of people across Canada and around the world. It has a network of branches in the U.S. and is eyeing further expansion. It rakes in billions in profits seemingly every year.

Here's a quick look at the dividend history over the last number of years:

Year	Dividend ($ per share)
1995	$ 0.59
1996	$ 0.67
1997	$ 0.76
1998	$ 0.88
1999	$ 0.94
2000	$ 1.14
2001	$ 1.38
2002	$ 1.52
2003	$ 1.72
2004	$ 2.02

As you can see, RBC is a great company that's in the habit of raising its dividend. For comparison, let's look at this in practical terms. If you would have bought Royal Bank shares on December 31, 1995, they would have cost you $15.56 each with a dividend of 59 cents. They would have paid you ($0.59 divided by $15.56) almost 4% a year which is still better than the interest on most savings accounts. In 2004, the dividend per share would have grown to $2.02 per share. You would be earning ($2.02 divided by $15.56) almost 13% a year on your original investment! The value of your shares would have also grown. In 2004, shares of RBC sold for over $60—four times what they were worth in 1995!

Once again, the important thing to focus on is the increasing dividends. These dividends should continue to increase for many years to come. This trend holds true for all the big banks. Royal Bank is just an example. In fact, each and every one of the big banks has been a good investment over time.

The Big Insurance Companies

The insurance companies are similar to the banks in that they have long operating histories and operate in the financial industry. Great-West Life, Sun Life, and Manulife are all good and each of them should increase their dividends regularly in the future. Personally, I like Manulife because it has significant exposure to the fast growing Asian market.

George Weston Limited

George Weston Limited is the majority owner of Loblaws which is the dominant grocery retailer in Canada. Founded in 1882, Weston also operates a number of bakeries across Canada and some in the United States. The company owns a very highly respected brand with President's Choice products and offers banking through a unit called President's Choice Financial. The company has a history of paying out ever increasing dividends and plowing the rest of the cash it generates back into buying and building more stores across the country. It's simple to understand and is impervious to economic downturns. Regardless of what happens to the overall economy, the simple fact is that everybody has to eat and Weston is in the food business.

The Weston family is the second richest family in Canada. Needless to say, they are great business people. The Loblaws stores are getting bigger and carrying a wider selection of merchandise over time. You get the feeling that the new Loblaws stores are not just supermarkets, but more like a main street in a box—a one-stop shop. You can get film developed, pick up prescription drugs, buy greeting cards for family members, pick up a bottle of wine, drop off your dry cleaning, do your banking, and of course do your grocery shopping. Overall, the stores are great, and the stock is too!

Corby Distilleries

Many of the regular consumer products Canadians purchase tend to be American. A trip down any store aisle reveals thousands of U.S. brands including Kraft, Coke, Pepsi, Doritos, and Post Cereal in food to Gillette, Johnson and Johnson, and Crest toothpaste in personal care products. The reality is that there are not too many Canadian consumer product companies that offer great investment opportunities. That's the result of being situated next to the largest economy in the world.

Although there are not many good consumer product companies to invest in, there are a few good ones. Corby Distilleries Limited, which is Canada's leading manufacturer and marketer of spirits, is one of them. Started in 1859, Corby produces many of Canada's most popular alcoholic drinks. Essentially Corby is a great company that throws off mountains of cash to shareholders by way of dividends. It is absolutely debt-free (which is a rarity), and pays an annual $2.00 dividend per share (which has just been raised to $2.20 while I'm sending this book to print). But it gets better. Corby can't figure out what to do with all the cash that piles up in its coffers, so every five years or so, it pays a whopping $16.50 special dividend (in addition to the regular dividend) to all its shareholders! Here's a quick look at how it's done over the last number of years—showing the dividends per share (regular and special):

Year	Regular (dividend)	Special (dividend)	Total (dividend)
1994	$ 1.12	$16.50	$17.62
1995	$ 1.15	nil	$ 1.15
1996	$ 1.24	nil	$ 1.24
1997	$ 1.28	nil	$ 1.28
1998	$ 1.70	$16.50	$18.20
1999	$2.00	nil	$ 2.00
2000	$2.00	nil	$ 2.00
2001	$2.00	nil	$ 2.00
2002	$2.00	nil	$ 2.00
2003	$2.00	nil	$ 2.00
Total Dividends Paid (1994–2003)			**$ 49.49**

At the close of 1994, the stock price was as low as $37.13. In the ten years since then, it's paid a total of $49.49 in dividends (see chart above). If you had bought the stock in 1994, you could have recovered all of your money and then some just by collecting the dividend every three months. The stock price has also climbed such that it's trading at around $65 a share at the time of this writing. Meanwhile, as the drinks keep flowing to the customers, the river of cash keeps flowing to the shareholders. Currently there is more cash accumulating in the company's vault. I wouldn't be surprised to see another special dividend being paid out in the next year or so. This is a stable business and a great investment.

Let's move on to a similar stock suggestion.

Rothmans Inc.

From a strictly investment point of view, Rothmans Inc. is a definite buy. Now I know that many people have an aversion to tobacco companies (due to ethical concerns), and that's understandable. However, if you happen to be a smoker and want to recoup some of the thousands you've spent on smoking, buying stock in Rothmans is a great way to do it. Rothmans is the second largest tobacco company in Canada with a market share of around 25% (and recently growing). The unique thing about Rothmans however, is that it is a market leader in the discount segment of the market with over 50% market share. Every year in Canada there's a decreasing number of smokers paying more taxes and higher prices for their habit. In the U.S. this has led to a huge increase in the sale of discount cigarettes and the same trend might play out in Canada. If it does, Rothmans is well positioned to take customers from its rivals and increase market share and profits over time.

Most people would consider tobacco a dying business, but annual price increases generally outweigh volume decreases, which drives profits up. To give you an example, suppose you're in a growing business and you increase sales. For every $1 increase in sales, the actual profit gain might be just a few pennies, because as you increased sales, you have to increase costs as well. Perhaps it's the cost of hiring new workers, building new factories, or channeling money into a new advertising campaign. In the case of Rothmans, they increase prices such that for every $1 increase in price they get a full $1 increase in profits! This is money that can go directly to shareholders. Rothmans doesn't need to spend any money on new factories or more workers and as a result, it doesn't know what to do with all the excess cash it generates. So it pays an annual dividend of $2 a share which represents a yield of about 6%. Even with the generous dividend the cash still piles up, so the company is also in the habit of paying out special dividends from time to time (just like Corby), which is more money in the pocket of its shareholders.

Rothmans is an even better stock because it operates in a no-growth industry, which means there will be few major competitors interested in entering the market. Advertising bans make it almost impossible for new entrants to gain any market share. Whenever negative news hits the U.S. tobacco industry, Rothmans falls in sympathy, which creates a buying opportunity. In 2003, you could have bought the stock for around $23 a share. It's paid more in dividends since 1993 (almost $25!) then it would have cost you to buy the stock. It's still accumulating cash at a furious pace. There should be many more dividend increases to go along with the steady supply of special dividends. There have been big headlines pertaining to lawsuits in the U.S., so this stock might be a little risky. I'd still say it's a lot safer than many technology stocks and it "shows you the money" on a regular basis.

Many people have ethical concerns regarding tobacco, so if you do, take a pass on this one. For those who already smoke, quit and use the money to buy the stock instead.

Mutual Fund Companies

It's interesting to note that many mutual fund company stocks have done much better than the actual funds they manage. There are three main publicly traded mutual fund companies in Canada. They are AGF Management Limited, C.I. Fund Management, and IGM Financial (formerly Investor's Group). These companies sell mutual funds to the public and collect the management expenses every year. Management fees range from less than 1% for some funds to around 3% for some specialty funds. There are billions of dollars invested in mutual funds in Canada and these companies are collecting their management fees on a lot of that money. It's a terrific business because as people keep investing more money each month, the amount collected in fees goes up as well. As a result, all of these companies generate torrents of cash, and they are in the habit of sending that cash to shareholders in the form of increasing dividends. Buy when the market hits a rough spot and then sit back and collect the dividends.

The investments mentioned above are just a few ideas. There are certainly others, but this should give you an idea of what sort of stocks to look for. Be careful to only buy quality firms that have shown an ability to give you more money in the form of dividends year after year. Also the above list overemphasizes financial stocks. This is because Canada derives a lot of its wealth from the resource sector. The old view of Canada as a "hewer of wood and drawer of water" although changing still has some truth to it. As a result of this, Canada is a prosperous country with a highly developed financial services sector and a lot of investment opportunities in this sector. However, most of the consumer products we tend to buy come from U.S. companies, so that limits our investment options somewhat.

For increased diversification, buy multinational American companies. To find good investments in this area, your first step should be to look at *Mergent's Handbook of High Dividend Achievers*. Here you will see a list of all the companies that have managed to increase their dividends for at least ten consecutive years. There are a number of companies that have managed to increase their dividends more than forty consecutive years! A company that can increase its dividend year after year is a strong one capable of withstanding a wide range of adversity. They come from a wide range of industries and most have been around for a very long time. They include companies like Coca Cola (drinks), Kraft (food), Citibank(financial services), Exxon Mobil (oil), Wal-Mart (retail), Wrigley (chewing gum), GE (many different businesses), McDonald's (fast food) Disney (entertainment), Gillette (personal care products), Tootsie Roll (candies), Budweiser (beer), and many, many others.

Another way of finding the best of the best American companies is to look at the book entitled *The 100 Best Stocks to Own in America.* This book is written by Gene Walden, and it gives the ranking of the 100 best companies to own. He also gives a brief description of each company with their individual earnings and dividend history.

Once you have a list of possible companies, decide in your mind if the product or service they offer is "recession-proof." If it's not, discard the company. Also think of your own perception of the company. Any company that you're not comfortable with is not worth owning.

Hint: Most of the best investments can be found with products you use every day.

Now you have a list of potential candidates. The next step is to look at *Value Line*. This is a service that covers most major companies in America and offers a brief write-up on what sort of business the company is in and other facts. It also shows many years of financial data for each company. It is available in a binder at many larger libraries or you can order it. It sounds complicated, but in reality, any ten-year-old could do research using this resource.

What exactly are you looking for? You want to see a strong history of rising dividends (this should already be the case as this is one of your initial selection criteria). You also want to see healthy rising earnings per share at least 10% a year on average. Another potential positive can be found when you look at the number of shares outstanding. You want to see the total number of shares getting smaller over time. This means that the company is buying back its own stock. The company is using some of the money it earns to buy out some of the existing shareholders. This is a very strong signal as it shows the company is cash rich and also interested in increasing shareholder wealth (that's your wealth).

The final step in the process is to check the price to make sure you are paying a fair price. The easiest way to do this is by looking at the stock price over the last number of years. If you see that the dividends and earnings have been rising, while the stock price has been falling, this is a good sign

Another method involves looking at the line graph at the top of the page (again in *Value Line*). It will show you the historical price ranges for the stock as well as a general average indicator of value (marked with a solid line). If the price of the stock falls substantially below this "value" line, it is an indication that it might be a good time to buy the stock. Try to buy stocks when the price is far below the *Value Line* solid line. Again, it's difficult to follow with words, but if you glance at the *Value Line* book for a minute, you'll understand it all perfectly. This method is simple enough for a child to follow, yet powerful enough that it allowed me to achieve early retirement.

Here's a specific example of a great American company that's been a wonderful long-term investment. Started in the 1880's, Johnson and Johnson is a huge manufacturer of health care products. You're probably familiar with the company through the Johnson's Baby products, but the company is much bigger than that. It operates in three main segments which include consumer products, pharmaceutical products and medical devices. The company consists of over 200 operating companies and sells products in over 175 countries around the world.

Johnson and Johnson is a rock in the foundation of the investment universe. It will probably be around for centuries. It's stable. In 2004 it raised it's dividend for the 42nd consecutive year! It's managed to increase sales for 70 consecutive years. It is next to impossible to imagine an event that would cripple a business like this. Here's the dividend history below:

Year	**Annual Dividend ($ U.S. per share)**
1993	$ 0.25
1994	$ 0.28
1995	$ 0.32
1996	$ 0.37
1997	$ 0.43
1998	$ 0.49
1999	$ 0.55
2000	$ 0.62
2001	$ 0.70
2002	$ 0.80
2003	$ 0.93
2004	$ 1.10

In 2004, Johnson raised its dividend again. It is on track to pay out $1.10 per share. You can see the general trend for dividends is up. Johnson's has been raising its dividend for longer than I have been alive and it'll still probably be doing it after I'm gone.

Johnson and Johnson is only one example of a great company to buy and hold. There are many other investment opportunities in the U.S. All you have to do is look for the high dividend achievers or read the book *The 100 Best Stocks to Own in America* then go to *Value Line* to see a company financial snapshot. You can also order annual reports (free of charge) directly from the companies.

In the next chapter we'll examine a recent stock purchase I made and go over the thinking process involved.

8

PUT YOUR MONEY WHERE YOUR MOUTH IS!

"With money in your pocket,
you are wise and you are handsome
and you sing well, too."
Yiddish Proverb

I want to show the basic thought process I go through when I'm buying a stock, so you have a framework to follow. This is a real example of a stock (Colgate Palmolive) I recently purchased and the factors I considered.

Colgate Palmolive has a few core areas including Oral care (toothpaste, etc), Personal Care (ex. Speed Stick deodorant), Household surface care (cleaners), Fabric care, and Pet Nutrition.

The first question you should ask is, "Is this company simple to understand?" Absolutely! They produce products that people use every day. You can't get too much easier than toothpaste. It's cheap to produce, sells for under a dollar, and its habit forming.

I'm sure you'd agree that brushing you teeth is a habit (after every meal!). So is deodorant—don't you use this every day? So the company has simple products that most people use.

But do people have brand loyalty? Let me ask you a question. When you buy deodorant, do you buy the first thing you see or do you have a certain brand you usually buy? Most people stick with one brand.

In toothpaste there are the two big brands—Crest and Colgate, along with a few smaller brands. If you see your regular brand of toothpaste selling for 99 cents, and you see another brand called "Super Cheap Toothpaste" selling for 89 cents, which one would you buy? In most cases teeth are considered very important to people, and they stick to the brand they trust—so the loyalty is high. In addition to this loyalty, the product is very recession-proof. You simply don't stop brushing your teeth because the economy is doing poorly.

Does it pay a dividend? Yes. At the time I was looking at it, the dividend was 96 cents a share. The shares sold for around $44, so the dividend was ($0.96 divided by $44) 2.1% (more than most savings accounts offer).

But what about the long-term performance? According to the annual report, Colgate has paid uninterrupted dividends since 1895! That means during the stock market crash of 1929, the great depression, the two world wars, the war in Vietnam, the cold war, the 1987 market crash...through it all, investors continued to receive their dividend cheques...without disruption!

In addition, the company has increased the dividend *every single year* for forty years! You get more money coming to you every year. As an example, in 1992 you could have bought shares for around $13 each. The dividends were 29 cents a share. Now the shares trade at around $45 and pay you 96 cents a share.

Here's another plus. It has large international operations. Its products are consumed in Latin America, Europe, Africa, and the fast growing Asian market. Colgate has also been investing money in China by adding to its manufacturing capacity and efficiency. This is a safe way to play the emergence of many new countries onto the world economic stage without taking undue risk.

It's also dominant. It has the leading market share in toothpaste in North America and in many of the other markets in the world where it operates. This is very important. Market share leaders can spend more on advertising than their competitors because these marketing costs are spread over a larger base of products. This allows them to keep gaining market share over time. Here's a simple example to explain this.

Suppose the toothpaste market is 100 tubes of toothpaste per year (to keep things simple) and each tube costs 10 cents to make and sells for $1. Suppose company A has a 50% market share while company B has a 5% share (we will ignore the other 45% of the market for this example, just to keep the math simple). Both Company A and B want to gain market share so they each spend aggressively ($10 total budget) on advertising. The cost of advertising per tube of toothpaste for each company is:

- Company A ($10 divided by 50 tubes = 20 cents a tube)
- Company B ($10 divided by 5 tubes = $2 a tube)

You can see that company B will be losing money on each tube of toothpaste sold because the marketing costs are simply too high! It would be spending $2 on each tube of toothpaste it sells (for only $1 each). It would be losing money on every tube it sold! Company A will only be spending 20 cents on each tube, and still making a profit. Eventually, company B will reduce its advertising budget to save money, and company A will get an ever increasing market share as it keeps its marketing efforts up. This is why you should always invest in the dominant companies. They usually become more dominant over time.

The final thing to look at is price. Colgate has been a great company for a long time, but you have to be patient and wait for an opportunity to get the investment cheaply. For example, you could have bought

Colgate in 1999 for $65 a share. In 1999, Colgate was still the great company it's always been, but it was overpriced. If you would have bought it then, five years later in 2004, you'd have lost a third of your money! So you have to wait until the market gives you your opportunity.

In September of 2004, that opportunity came. Colgate announced it was only going to earn around 57 cents a share instead of the 68 cents it was projected to earn. Why? Higher costs including higher marketing costs! The company was spending more on marketing—investing for the future! With that notorious short-term focus many investors are renowned for, the shares lost almost 12%. Then they kept dropping lower and lower each day. I managed to get some for around $44 with a stable, secure dividend of 96 cents (as mentioned earlier).

What's the secret to finding them while they're cheap? Simple. Look for negative headlines. I hadn't been following the stock price every day for years and waiting for my chance to buy it. I just happened to be looking at a newspaper when I saw a brief article showing Colgate as a "dog" (a term for a bad performing investment). I knew about Colgate toothpaste, but not much else about the company. So while doing groceries that day, I looked at a tube of Colgate toothpaste. It had a 1-800 number on it, so I went to a payphone in the store and told them to send me the most recent annual report. It cost me nothing. When I read through the report a week or so later (after receiving it), I found that it fit my criteria of a good stock (outlined in the last chapter). The stock price had fallen a little more since I had read the article in the newspaper, and it seemed reasonably priced, so I bought it.

One thing worth noting—I have terrible short term timing! The stock price fell a little more after I bought it, but that doesn't matter. Whenever I buy an investment, the price always seems to move down further for a while. This has always happened, so I'm used to it. Despite this fact, I've still managed to retire early and my investments have done very well over the long term. So don't worry about the short term ups and downs of the stock market.

What's the strategy now? Am I waiting for the next quarter or two to show improvement so I can sell them and make money? No! My plan now is to hold onto them and collect my ever increasing dividend cheques. Since Colgate has been paying these dividends for over 100 years (since 1895), it's a safe bet that they'll continue. With over forty consecutive years of dividend increases, we can assume that the amount of these cheques being sent to shareholders will increase over time. I don't care what the stock price does! Why should you care about the irrational behaviour of the stock market?

Now let's consider a "worst case scenario." The stock market crashes just like it did starting in 1929 (it loses over 90% of its value). Now what happens?

The price of the stock would fall from $45 to just over $4. Initially, I might not be very happy. But then what? If you turn on the T.V. and see that the stock market crashes, does that make you stop brushing your teeth? No! So the company keeps on selling its toothpaste regardless of the stock market.

Let's assume the shares stay at $4 each. Right now, Colgate spends over $1 billion dollars every year buying back its own shares. What this means is that they buy the shares and retire them. To illustrate this, suppose you are in business. There are 10 partners, you and nine others. Every year, the company gives some money to one partner and buys his share. So each year there is one fewer partner. After nine years, you'd own the whole company. This is what Colgate essentially does. Current shareholders are being bought out. If the stock price stayed at $4 and Colgate kept spending $1 billion a year to buy back shares, it could buy back almost half the company every year. After a little over two years you'd own the whole company!

So stock market crashes are the friend of the person wanting to invest more money. Even if you're at the stage where you are retired and just harvesting your "fruit" (dividends) every year, a market crash still helps you. This is because these great companies are usually buying back more of their own shares over time (and increasing the amount of the business you own). So watch the stock market just as you watch the signs displaying the price of gasoline outside of gas stations—and react the same way. When the price goes up, mutter obscenities under your breath, if it goes down, smile—if it goes *way down,* rejoice!

But in reality you'll probably never be that lucky. You can pray for a great stock market crash and hope to party like it's 1929, but you will probably never be that fortunate.

Once again, when do I plan to sell these shares?

Never!

9

LOCATION. LOCATION. LOCATION.

"Land. They're not making any more of the stuff."!

Will Rogers

My first introduction to the idea of investing in land came when I was seven years old. I think my mom had bought the game Monopoly—which according to Hasbro, is the world's most popular board game. It was invented by Charles B. Darrow in 1933, during the great depression.

As soon as I played it once I was hooked. Every day after school I would race home to play. If we went over to my Uncle and Aunt's place, I would try to corral them into playing. I loved the game. As I continued to pester everyone around me into playing Monopoly, my mom began to call it "Monotony." I didn't really understand why she had trouble pronouncing the name of the game but I really didn't care as long as we could play it. It took me a few years to figure out what she had been trying to say.

Although I was a little slow at picking up on her play on words, I was quick at getting the main strategy of the game. Buy real estate and try to build on it. I also realized the railroads offered more cash up front and required less investment before they began to bear fruit, so they were a good foundation. They were sort of like the "show me the money now!" investments. I also noticed that the winner wasn't necessarily the person who passed "Go" the most. Isn't this true in real life? Most of us spend our time "passing Go" as in collecting our paychecks, but if you want to become financially independent, you have to invest in something. And the idea of owning my own land appealed to me.

There's something reassuring about investing in land and buildings. Wars are usually fought for real estate as countries want more land. North America was settled by huge waves of immigrants who came to our shores in search of the proverbial pot of gold and the end of the rainbow—free land! Go to Toronto or Vancouver and look at the price of a small piece of land downtown and you'll quickly see just how valuable land can be. Many fortunes have been made by investing in real estate. It's a great way to have money working for you. Isn't it wonderful to just think about owning something like an apartment, store, or warehouse and just collecting the rent cheque every month. If you had a few of these, you could just drive around once a month and pick up your cheques and you would never have to worry about money again.

But of course, there's a downside. If you rented out a house or apartment, what do you do if your tenant calls you at 2 am to tell you their toilet is clogged? You have to scramble out of bed and go fix it. What if they decide not to pay? You can evict them, but that takes time and the process is cumbersome. What if you rent it to someone and they trash it? What if the furnace breaks? When does the roof need to be fixed? The washer broke.

Forget it! Too much trouble!

You could invest in commercial real estate, but that requires lots of money. A recession might hit and your tenant goes out of business leaving you with a vacant property and the mortgage and taxes to pay. Should you forget real estate?

Real Estate is a great long term investment that is tangible and tends to appreciate in price. Land becomes more valuable over time as it benefits from inflation and the fact that the population tends to increase. If you want to get an idea of how it appreciates, ask someone who bought a house thirty years ago what they originally paid for it. Real estate can be a spectacular investment but can also be a pain. How can you get the benefit from real estate as an investment without having the burden of real estate ownership? Here's what you can do—buy a REIT.

REITs (short for Real Estate Investment Trust) are entities similar to businesses that own a lot of real estate. There are unit holders, the same as shareholders in stocks, and they each own a tiny piece of the company. The company in turn owns many properties across the country, so you can see which properties you own around your city. With each property you effectively own a tiny piece of it. With REITs, look at the list of all the properties and imagine that you own one or two bricks of each building. You're also entitled to a small amount of the rent from each place.

There are several advantages to this structure. First, it's hands off. You don't manage any of the properties. You are just the owner! There is a management team, the same as with a corporation. They deal with the day to day operations like unclogging toilets, collecting rent, regular maintenance, getting tenants, buying and selling buildings, and arranging financing. They collect the rent every month and then give some of it to all the unit holders. You simply wait for the money to appear in your brokerage account every month and then spend it.

Another advantage is the fact that you own one or two bricks of each building rather than one whole building. This way, if there's a problem with one of the buildings and it can't be rented out for whatever reason, it doesn't really affect you. It's only one building in a portfolio of many. It's safer. The buildings are located all over the country, so a recession in Calgary due to the collapse of the price of oil won't have dire consequences on your properties in Toronto—it smoothes the business cycle out.

The final advantage is that often the income is tax advantaged (you pay less tax on it). You might earn $1,000 of income in a year, but only have to pay tax on some of it. In other words, if you worked and earned $1,000, you would have much less in your pocket to spend *after tax* than if you earned $1,000 from your REIT! Talk about having your cake and eating it too!

There are various kinds of REITs. These include apartment (where people live), office (where many people work), warehouse (for storage), Hotels, Retirement (nursing homes and the like), and Commercial (retail stores).

It's best to avoid residential REITs for the simple reason that you never know if or when the provincial governments are going to reinstate rent control. With rent control, there is no way to increase your income quickly or even ensure that the rent charged covers the costs.

Office REITs are another option, but not a good one. They are susceptible to economic downturns and layoffs. You only have to look at how vacancy rates exploded in some cities right after the technology meltdown to understand the potential risks. These empty office buildings weren't providing any rental income to their owners.

Warehouse REITs are another area to not invest in. Even though storage space is always needed, more can be built very easily and location is not really all that important to potential customers, so new competing buildings can be built at any time.

Hotel REITs are also dangerous. The hotel industry can be very cyclical, moving up and down with the general economy. If you look at the performance of hotel companies after the terrorist attack on the World Trade Center on September 11th, you can fully appreciate this.

You're probably beginning to wonder why I started this chapter extolling the virtues of real estate investment trusts, but I don't seem to like any of them. This is one very important key to investing successfully and that is to always be very choosy. I do like retirement REITs. Simply put, North America is aging and the demand for accommodation for seniors is increasing, so this is a good area to be invested in.

REIT recommendation #1: Retirement Residences REIT

Retirement Residences Real Estate Investment Trust is well positioned for the future growth in demand for senior accommodations. It pays a pretty sizeable distribution of $0.84 per unit and the units are priced around $9.80 each. That gives a yield of over

($0.84 divided by $9.80) 8.5%. In addition, a large portion of the distribution is not taxed when you receive it. In 2003, over 80% of the distribution was taxed deferred. In other words, if you worked and earned income in Ontario you'd pay about 22% tax (at the lowest rate) and approximately 7% in other deductions. In total you would keep about 71 cents on every dollar you earned. If you collected distributions from this REIT, you'd only pay tax on one fifth of the amount you receive, so you'd be paying less than 5% tax! It's a little risky because it has only been a REIT for a few years and it has reduced its distribution once. If you want something less risky, look at the next suggestion.

Finally commercial REITs can be great. These are investments which include various forms of commercial real estate like shopping malls and big box stores. Once you've built a large neighbourhood mall, the chances are remote that someone else will build a competing one—it just wouldn't make economic sense. In addition, all of the available land might already be used up. In this kind of REIT, location is important!

In addition, although retailers' profits are affected by economic downturns, if you focus on property with strong retailers who are not affected that much by the economy like supermarkets (people always have to eat) or Wal-Mart (king of discounters), you should find yourself with a stable money machine. This leads me to:

REIT recommendation #2:
Riocan Real Estate Investment Trust

Riocan is a wonderful investment. It owns many retail properties across Canada. It has one of the highest stability ratings (safety of distribution) for REITs from Standard and Poor's (which determines the safety of distributions for various trusts in Canada). Riocan leases property to some of the largest names in retail including Wal-Mart, Loblaws, Zellers, Shoppers Drug Mart, and many more. It tries to find tenants that are national or international in scope to add further stability. Distributions have gone up annually since 1994, almost tripling! Here's a quick peek at the payout history:

Year	Distribution ($ per share)
1994	$ 0.43
1995	$ 0.58
1996	$ 0.65
1997	$ 0.78
1998	$ 0.95
1999	$ 1.04
2000	$ 1.07
2001	$ 1.08
2002	$ 1.11
2004	$ 1.14
Total Distributions	**$8.83**

In 2004, it's expected that Riocan will pay a distribution at a rate of $1.20 per unit. The units are trading at $15.75 each at the time of this writing, so that means they yield roughly 7.6%. You could have bought the units for less than $8.00 in early 2000 or under $5.00 each in 1995. If you had bought at these prices, the current yield would have been over 15% and 24% respectively on your original investment! This is a secure investment and highly recommended if you can wait for an opportunity to scoop it up at the right price. Adding some real estate investments to your portfolio is a great way to increase the cash flow your portfolio is generating and can bring you that much closer to an early retirement. Just remember to be choosy and wait patiently for the right price. The next chapter will look at other investments that pay high and stable distributions.

10

ELECTRIFY YOUR PORTFOLIO!

"Benjamin Franklin may have discovered electricity, but it was the man who invented the meter who made the money."

Earl Wilson

If you've ever paid any utility bills then you realize how expensive they can be. Unfortunately if you spend a lot on energy for your home, there is not too much you can do to reduce the costs except conservation. If you are short of money you can easily decide to eat at home and bring your lunch to work. You can also decide not to buy a new car and make do with the old one a little longer. Bypass the coffee shop you like so much. Postpone the trip to the warm sunny island you've been thinking about. There are so many ways you can tighten your belt if you absolutely have to. But you can't go without energy in your home. The fact is that most of us need energy for our day to day lives. We can't avoid this expense. This inescapable fact is precisely what makes pipeline and energy trusts such great investments. Regardless of the season, economy, or fashion, people need power to live. The two kinds of trusts that you can invest in that will add a solid foundation to your portfolio and help you reach early retirement are pipeline and power generation trusts.

Building a pipeline is a very expensive investment. You have to hire many workers and use a lot of expensive machinery to construct the pipeline which could be thousands of kilometers long. It can take years to complete one. This time and expense factor is actually an advantage when you look at pipelines as an investment. Once you own one, others are unlikely to build another one until demand increases enough to justify it because it wouldn't make economic sense. Once you own a pipeline, you merely collect your profits as the gas or oil is constantly pumped through it.

Historically pipeline or utility companies were considered "widows and orphans" stocks because they were so stable and ran almost no risk of going out of business, so they were suitable for people who could not afford to lose any money. Recently, some of these stocks have been converted into investment trusts. These are taxed advantaged investments and they pay out very high distributions in most cases. These can help you retire earlier because they pay you a high yield right away. A few of these are highlighted below, but if you research these on your own, you can come up with others.

Recommended Pipeline Trust #1:
Pembina Pipeline Income Fund

Pembina Pipeline trades on the Toronto Stock Exchange. It began operating as a trust in 1997. I know that one of the investment tenets is to only buy investments with a long operating history, but this trust was operating privately before it was converted into a trust. In addition, the economics of pipelines (mentioned above) coupled with the high stability rating given by Standard and Poor's allow this to be a great candidate for any conservative portfolio. It owns a number of pipelines in western Canada which transport oil and natural gas liquids. A quick look at its annual report shows that it has been a consistent distribution payer. As of this writing, it is paying $1.05 per unit annually and the units are trading at around $12.00 which offers a yield of almost 9% ($1.05 divided by $12). You wouldn't expect the unit price to increase much over time. This is the sort of investment where you only expect to receive stable distributions year after year.

This sort of investment is also offered for a cheap price from time to time. Early in 2000, when the market was enthralled with high technology stocks, you could have picked these units up for around $6.00 each. With the current yield of $1.05, that means you'd be getting a return on your original investment of 17.5% ($1.05 divided by $6) every year! Wait patiently and try to scoop them up when they're cheap. Then hold onto them forever.

Recommended Pipeline Trust #2:
Enbridge Income Fund

The main asset in the Enbridge Income fund is the Alliance pipeline. This is a huge pipeline that starts in Canada and goes along 3000 km to the U.S.A. The Enbridge Income Fund has a 50% interest in the Canadian portion. The fund also holds an interest in some pipelines in Saskatchewan. The fund is rated very high for stability, and should provide unit holders with safe distributions for quite some time. Right now, the units are yielding almost 8%.

Power generation trusts are also a great type of investment that can add stability and additional cash flow to your portfolio. Regardless of various factors, people need electricity. As the overall population grows, electricity consumption also increases over time. Here are a couple of power trusts that can help your portfolio:

Recommended Power Generation Trust #1: Algonquin Power Income Fund

Algonquin Power Income Fund is predominantly a hydroelectric power producer. Hydroelectric energy is generated by the flow of water. As long as the rivers continue to flow, power is produced.

Algonquin has added some gas powered generators, biomass generators, and also some water distribution facilities for further diversification. Algonquin is also acquiring plants all over North America which means that low water levels in one area might be offset by higher levels in another area. In addition, hydroelectric power is an environmentally friendly source of electricity, which has become important as countries wrestle with pollution issues.

The fund pays out $0.92 per unit. As I write this, the units are trading at around $9.25. It is very stable and the yield works out to almost 10%. In addition, you don't have to pay tax on a large portion of the distribution as long as you hold onto the units as this part is tax deferred.

Recommended Power Generation Trust #2: Trans Canada Power

Trans Canada Power is partially owned by Trans Canada Pipelines. This trust has many gas fired power generation facilities and has the highest stability rating possibly given by Standard and Poor's. Remember, Standard and Poor's is a company that provides risk assessment and credit ratings for corporations and similar entities. It also provides stability ratings for trusts. This means that the distributions paid by Trans Canada are very safe. It has increased its stability by entering into long-term electricity sales contacts and also long-term fuel contracts. It is a reliable, income generating asset that pays close to 8% at the time of this writing.

The investment ideas listed above are by no means the only great investments in this area. Adding some of these types of investments to your portfolio can greatly increase your annual cash flow. The payouts are high and generally stable. This type of investment is meant to start putting money in your pocket right away and bringing you a few years closer to escaping the dependence on employment income.

11

BLACK GOLD, EH?

"The meek shall inherit the earth,
but not its mineral rights."
J. Paul Getty

Oil has been a source of wealth for many people in the past. Rockefeller created Standard Oil in the U.S., and was the richest man in that country at the time of his death. K.C. Irving created a business empire up here in Canada with the help of the oil industry. Saudi Arabia and many other oil rich nations have reaped tremendous rewards merely because they were endowed with large quantities of oil. Right here in Canada, the only province with a claim of debt free status is oil rich Alberta. The other provincial governments can only look at Alberta and wish they had such resources.

The importance of oil goes beyond transportation. It is used in the manufacture of many things we use ranging from plastics to pharmaceuticals. Oil is the very foundation of modern society and is arguably the most important commodity in the world today. To put it bluntly, without oil, we as a society would be thrown back to a lifestyle similar to that of the middle ages.

Some experts feel that we are going to hit "peak world oil" where production simply will not be able to be increased any further and will begin to decline. I have also read that many companies and countries have intentionally overstated their true oil reserves (the amount of oil they own that's still in the ground) for their own interests. If oil companies overstate reserves, it can drive their share prices artificially higher. Apparently countries in OPEC (Organization of Petroleum Exporting Countries) have an incentive to overstate reserves because their production quotas are based on their reserve estimates.

To add further thought on the potential strain on oil supplies, think for a minute about what is happening in the world. Right now Canada, the U.S., Europe, Japan, and a few other countries are considered "developed." These countries have about 1 billion people *in total* or less than a quarter of the world's population. These people drive cars, take vacations, buy lots of products, and because of this lifestyle consume enormous amounts of oil per person compared to the rest of the world. Currently, China and India are developing very quickly. These countries have over 1 billion people *each* or a total of almost 2.5 billion people. What will happen when all these billions of people begin to consume oil on the same scale that we are used to here in North America?

China used to be a net exporter of oil. Now they are set to overtake Japan as the world's second biggest importer of oil, while the vast majority of the Chinese population is still living a very primitive peasant existence. What all this boils down to is that over the long term, oil demand is going to increase relentlessly.

On the supply side, as we use more oil, there's less of it left to be used because once you consume oil, it's gone forever. This is an important fact. With gold for example, it never gets "used up." People merely melt it down and reuse it over time. So as more gold gets mined, the total supply in existence increases. This fact is simply not true for oil. In addition, the size of new oil finds around the globe is getting smaller as the "easy to find" oil has already been found!

What's the situation like with oil's close cousin—natural gas? Here in North America we essentially have a domestic natural gas market. That means we produce all the natural gas we need. We're fortunate in that we have been endowed with enormous natural gas resources. We have pipelines crisscrossing the continent, transporting it. Most newly built homes are heated with natural gas. It's clean burning and up until recently has been relatively cheap. Many electricity generation plants use natural gas to produce electricity. In recent years there have been a number of gas fired generation plants coming on stream as the demand for electricity rises—using increasing amounts of natural gas.

U.S. natural gas production has been falling since the 1970's. They have been importing increasing amounts from Canada and Mexico over time. But Canadian and Mexican gas production has its limits. Natural gas is similar to oil in the sense that once you've used it, it's gone forever. Recent discussions in North America have focused on importing natural gas.

How do you import natural gas? First you have to cool it down into liquid form. Then you send it by ship to the country which is importing it where it is restored into gas form. Not many people want LNG (liquefied natural gas) terminals in their back yards. In addition, these terminals are expensive to build and take years to complete. Importing natural gas is a very complex and expensive proposition. The price of natural gas would have to be high enough to justify this sort of investment. The fact that some major oil and gas companies are looking at building terminals in North America tells me that natural gas is probably going to be more expensive in the future than it has been in the past.

We're headed for higher energy prices! It's not a pretty picture for consumers. If you retire and you're on a fixed income trying to pay these ever escalating energy bills, what do you do? Energy is a necessary expense. You can't avoid it. You can conserve a little, but you definitely can't avoid using it altogether. So what can you do?

The answer is to become a producer. Now I'm not saying that you should go out and start drilling for oil or natural gas. But you should invest in energy in some way. Everyone thinking of retiring should have some exposure to energy because each and every one of us is an energy consumer. The simplest way to make sure that we don't suffer a hit to our lifestyle in retirement because of higher energy costs is to ensure that we also benefit from higher energy costs. If we own some energy investments, even though our costs to fill up the car or the costs to heat our homes might go up, we will benefit because the investments we've made will be reaping the rewards of the increased prices.

Simply stated, if your energy costs go up over time, the money you get from your energy investments in the form of dividends or distributions will go up as well to offset your increased costs.

But where should you invest? First let me ask you a

quick question. Which country do you think is the biggest energy supplier to the U.S.? Saudi Arabia? Iraq? The correct answer is Canada. Canada is blessed with large quantities of oil and natural gas. Canada has the second largest oil reserves in the world—right after Saudi Arabia! Clearly Canada is an energy producing powerhouse! As such there are ample areas for you to choose to invest in. Below are a few possibilities.

Recommended Royalty Trust #1: Pengrowth Energy Trust

Pengrowth Energy is a royalty trust that has various conventional oil and natural gas assets across Canada. It began operating in 1988 and has a great track record of paying out lots of cash to unit holders. Distribution yields commonly fluctuate between 12% and 15% annually. Being an oil and gas trust, the one thing you have to remember is that it is pumping oil and gas out of the ground and selling it, then giving you a portion of the profits. Eventually all the oil and natural gas will be gone. To rectify this, Pengrowth routinely buys new oil and gas properties from various companies that operate in Canada, thus replacing this oil and gas. The track record of replacing its reserves has been quite good over time. The distribution history has been fantastic. Let's take a look:

Year	Distribution ($ per share)
1989	$ 0.48
1990	$ 0.72
1991	$ 0.84
1992	$ 0.68
1993	$ 1.18
1994	$ 1.12
1995	$ 1.35
1996	$ 1.67
1997	$ 2.11
1998	$ 1.65
1999	$ 2.22
2000	$ 3.55
2001	$ 3.49
2002	$ 1.93
2003	$ 2.66
Total distributions	**$25.65**

The first thing you should notice is that the distributions from this royalty trust fluctuate a lot. This volatility in distributions is mainly related to the underlying prices of oil and natural gas. If these prices go up, the amount of cash the oil and gas trust generates goes up and vice versa. This part of your portfolio is mostly a hedge against rising oil and gas prices. If you are on a fixed income from your portfolio, you want to minimize the effects of rapidly rising oil and/or gas prices. This type of royalty trust accomplishes this beautifully.

In addition, because of the volatility of oil and gas prices, there are great opportunities to pick these units up at fire sale prices from time to time. For example, these units traded as low as $ 4.00 per share in 1992. That means you would have paid only $4 for each unit, but collected over $23 in distributions! This is a phenomenal rate of return. If oil and gas prices are indeed headed higher over the long term, this trust should do very well.

If you would prefer an energy trust that doesn't have to rely on continually making new acquisitions to increase supply then consider the following,

Recommended Royalty Trust #2:
Canadian Oil Sands Trust

Canadian Oil Sands Trust owns about a 35% share of Syncrude, which is a consortium of oil producers that include the biggest names in Canada such as Petro-Canada and Imperial Oil (Esso). Syncrude has a producing life span of 35 years and they estimate the life span could be increased to over 50 years! The amount of oil trapped in these sands is greater than the amount of oil most countries have in total!

The oil industry has known that oil existed there for a long time, but it took a while to develop the technology to extract the oil economically. The oil sands are not a conventional source of oil. They contain deposits of bitumen, a heavy black oil that has to be processed into crude oil before it can be used by refineries. They've built a tremendous amount of infrastructure to do this over the last several years. Now, every barrel of oil that is produced by Syncrude sends some cash to Canadian Oil Sands Trust, which is then sent to the investors. There are billions of barrels of oil trapped there. For unit holders, it's like money in the bank—sort of like your own personal "oil bank."

There is also speculation that the U.S. might become even more interested in oil coming from Canada. Geopolitically, the U.S. is vulnerable because they rely so heavily on oil from the Middle East, which has historically been a very unstable area. What would happen if there were terrorist attacks on some major oil infrastructure targets in Saudi Arabia? How high would the price of oil climb? Some argue that increasing reliance on Canada would increase energy security for the world's largest economy.

There is one concern with the oil sands. They rely heavily on natural gas for processing the oil. In other words if natural gas prices were to skyrocket while oil prices were to drop, this trust would be hurt. The way to counteract this is to also buy some shares in a natural gas producer such as Encana. This Canadian company is the largest independent natural gas producer in North America. This would help offset the possibility of a huge natural gas price increase.

Recommended Hedge for Canadian Oil Sands:
Encana

The main point is that we are all consumers of energy. If you want to protect yourself from rising energy costs over time, the safest way is for you to buy some energy exposure. This way if prices go up, even though you pay more at the pumps as a consumer, you reap the rewards as an investor. The goal is for the investment income increase to offset the price increases faced by you as a consumer.

12

HOW DO YOU START?

"All I ask is the chance to prove that money can't make me happy."
Spike Milligan

Before we go on, I would like to touch upon the fact that trust units (covered in the last three chapters), pay large tax deferred distributions, but there is no guarantee the government will allow this beneficial tax treatment to continue. There are a lot of retirees collecting these distributions though, so this is an area where politicians will probably tread carefully. The distributions should remain generous, but the tax policies related to these investments *might* change. In addition, many trusts don't have limited liability like corporations do. Some provinces are in the process of granting it (and Alberta already has), but at the time of this writing they have not completed the process for this. Trusts usually carry insurance, but you should be aware of all these factors before investing.

So far we've looked at how to invest. If you've already built up a nest egg, then the previous chapters show you how to invest your money safely and efficiently to reach early retirement.

But what if you don't already have money to invest? What if your income is not very high? How can you come up with the money you need to start down the path to retirement?

That's the focus of the next few chapters. I'll give you a summary of my path to early retirement followed by some information on simplifying spending, saving money on your housing costs, reducing debt, and tax saving ideas. These steps will help you save up the money to invest. Finally we'll look at the advantages and disadvantages of RRSPs.

13

FINANCIALLY FREE BY 35! MY JOURNEY RETRACED

"There's no security in life, only opportunity."
Douglas Macarthur

My retirement journey started in 1992. This is when I implemented a regular savings plan and started putting aside $200 a month into mutual funds. I was 22 at the time.

I graduated from university in 1993. I had chosen to study accounting "yawn!" realizing only in my final year that it wasn't the appropriate degree for me. I hated it! I decided that a career in this area just wasn't in the cards for me.

I had paid for my tuition myself with earnings from summer jobs, so I graduated with a small amount of money saved and no debt! I decided to work part time for about 10 months and then I headed to Europe for backpacking the following summer.

Upon my return I decided I didn't want to pursue the standard career path. My goal was to leave the Canadian wintry cold behind and head to Australia in early January. I wanted to spend a year there. So I found another part-time job. My dad just sort of looked at me and asked, "So what exactly is it that you want to do with your life anyhow?" I tried to explain to him that I was saving $200 every month and investing it all in mutual funds. I was also adding any additional money I received like the quarterly GST credit or my income tax return. I had read *The Wealthy Barber*, and was convinced that if I just kept to my savings plan that I wouldn't have to worry about my future. I could travel and do what I wanted while building up my financial nest egg. So before I left for Australia, true to myself I deposited $2,400 into my brokerage account to pay for the year I was going to be away. I paid myself first a year in advance. Now I was free to spend the rest of my money on whatever I wanted to do in Australia knowing that I had already met my monthly commitment to myself.

As already mentioned earlier, I had read various investment books (most of which are on my recommended list at the back of the book), and had decided to buy some stocks by myself, doing my own research. This allowed me to get an even better rate of return on my investments.

Going off to Australia and New Zealand was truly amazing. The entire year was spectacular. I was able to do so many things ranging from scuba diving, white water rafting, and skydiving, to learning to throw boomerangs and making fires the way the aborigines had done it. All too soon the year was over and I had to go back to Ottawa. Touching down on the icy runway in Ottawa on Christmas Eve, I found myself in –25 degree weather. I decided to head to Vancouver about a week later.

Vancouver was difficult because it's such an expensive city to live in. I had gone into debt on my credit cards doing all the things I had wanted to do in my travels. Now while living in Vancouver, I had these debts to pay and I was unemployed. My investment account had done very well while I had been away, so I could have easily cashed out some of my stocks and paid off my debts, but I refused to do this. I had made a rule with myself that my brokerage account was a one-way account. I had to put money in every month, but I could never take any out until I had reached my goal of having enough to retire on forever. So I looked for work in Vancouver. I found nothing.

After about three desperate weeks of searching, I accepted the worst job I have ever had. I worked for a telemarketing firm earning roughly $6/hour. I barely scraped by. I only paid rent and food, with absolutely nothing left over. I held steadfast and refused to dip into my investment account. I finally got another telemarketing job working for $10/hour selling long distance packages. At the beginning of many shifts the supervisor would say that if you didn't sell at least two new plans, you would lose your job. It wasn't very much fun.

I had continued searching and finally received a call from Revenue Canada for a temporary job processing tax returns. About one week later I received another call. I had applied to BC Tel and had gone to a series of interviews. I could also start working for them. I still had all the debt I had incurred in my travels. Another kind of debt was also piling up, but many people wouldn't consider this a true debt. Since university I had vowed to myself that regardless of the situation, I would always pay myself $200/month. I was many months in arrears (to myself) at this stage. I made a decision right then. I would work at both Revenue Canada and BC Tel until I paid off all my credit card debts as well as all the debt I owed to myself. If I didn't keep paying myself each and every month, I would not progress towards my goal of financial independence.

Every morning for six weeks I woke up at 5:30 am to go to work at the Taxation Centre in Surrey (about 1 hour away). I started work at 7:00 am. When I finished at 3:00 pm I would again hop on the Sky Train (Vancouver's above ground train system) and go to my job at BC Tel. I would work from 4:00 pm until 9:30 pm and then take the Sky Train home by 10:30 pm. It was a very tiring routine, but I did it and got out of debt. I also caught up on all my missed payments to myself.

Once I achieved all this, I quit working for Revenue Canada. I started having a lot more fun—going on boating trips, scuba diving trips, and hiking trips. After the summer was over I wanted to do some more traveling but I didn't have any money. Again, I could have used some money from my investment account, but I refused to touch it. So I decided to teach English in Asia. A friend who happened to be teaching in Korea at the time led me there. I called a number he had given me and within three weeks I had quit my job at BC Tel and was boarding an airplane to South Korea—a country that is still technically at war with North Korea.

In Korea I had many wonderful experiences. I tried many different kinds of food, became proficient with chopsticks, got my black belt in Taekwondo, and learned how to speak Korean well enough to do all the things I needed to do while living there. But the most important thing that happened is that I met Hyeeun (pronounced Hay Un), my future wife. We got married in a typical Korean wedding and had a one month honeymoon in Bali, Indonesia.

Bali is a tropical paradise that offers everything an island traveler could want with the added benefit of being very affordable. We rented a beach house which consisted of one bedroom with a queen sized bed, ceiling fan and an attached bathroom. It cost $5 a night and included a fruit pancake breakfast every morning for the two of us. We went out to see the dolphins, snorkeled, swam, and went white water rafting.

After finishing in Korea we headed back to Canada. All this time I continued to transfer $200 each and every month to my brokerage account.

The point of retracing my journey is fourfold. Number one is to illustrate the fact that I never earned an extremely high salary. In most cases I earned substantially less than the average Canadian salary. You simply don't need to earn big bucks to retire early, although that could make your journey a little faster.

The second point is that although I did sacrifice to reach my goal, I didn't live a miserly existence. I traveled and experienced many new things while still saving up for my early retirement.

The third point is that I didn't budget or worry about where every penny was spent, but I faithfully paid myself every month. This is of absolute importance if you want to escape the rat race and retire. Even during times where I didn't have a high enough income to make the payment to myself, I would record the debt as outstanding and pay myself whenever I got the money.

Finally, although I started off by contributing regularly to mutual funds, my strategy evolved over time. I kept some mutual funds but started adding well-researched, safe common stocks. This was an important strategy and it accelerated the whole process of early retirement.

Was this plan difficult? Sure it was, but it seemed better than working 25 or 30 years longer than I wanted. The sacrifice was absolutely worth it!

The following chapters will look at ways in which you can save some money to invest without hurting your lifestyle.

14

SIMPLIFY YOUR SPENDING

"Why pay a dollar for a bookmark?
Why not use the dollar for the bookmark?"
Steven Spielberg

The concept of simplifying your spending is crucial if you want to retire as early as possible. This process helps you on two fronts. First, the less you spend, the more you save and the quicker you can reach the promised land of financial independence where money works for you instead of you working for money. Second, simplifying spending lowers how much money you need to live on. If you can increase the efficiency of how you spend your money, you will need less and therefore be able to retire earlier.

The key here is to find a way to spend less without depriving yourself. This idea is similar to driving a fuel-efficient vehicle versus a gas guzzler. Both will get you to your destination, but one will do it using a lot less resources than the other.

Spending Idea #1:

Simplifying spending should not be a form of self-deprivation.

Not only would depriving yourself of the things you want out of life not be fun, but you wouldn't do it for very long. Think of all the people in North America who are overweight and the billions of dollars spent dieting and other programs by people trying to lose weight. How many people lose weight and keep it off permanently? Very few do. The key is to find things you enjoy doing and use that to reach your goals. I find the people who can't wait for the snow to come so that they can go skiing or who can't wait for the snow to melt so that they can go biking are the ones who successfully stay in shape. It's not a chore for them. It's enjoyment! If something is too painful or becomes a burden then you won't keep at it. Humans are designed to seek pleasure and avoid pain. Setting up an exercise routine that is painful is setting up something that you are designed to avoid. It's the same with depriving yourself to save money. It's just not going to work!

Another key fact is to remember that simplifying spending is NOT budgeting. Some people can use budgeting very effectively. Most can't. I'm one of those people who can't. Budgeting seems to be like creating a workout routine. Many people spend time and devise a very involved plan but after a short time they find it too difficult to follow and simply stop. Budgeting does not work for the vast majority of people. Also, who really wants to sit down and analyze where every dollar goes every month? It all sounds pretty boring to me. If budgeting works for you, great! Keep doing it. For the rest of us, let's look at another simpler way.

Spending Idea #2:

Budgeting does NOT work for most people.

The basic framework of this strategy involves dividing your spending into two categories, "essential and non-essential." It would look like the illustration below:

Essential	Non-essential

Essential spending includes the necessities like food, mortgage payments, clothing, etc. These are the items that you can't live without. It's the non-essential items that hold the key to retiring early. Go to your non-essential list and create two sub-lists. Divide your non-essential costs into "life-enhancing" and non life-enhancing" like I've done below:

Essential	**Non-essential**

Life-enhancing	Non life-enhancing

What does life-enhancing and non life-enhancing mean? Let me explain with a couple examples.

My family enjoys using the internet, which is non-essential. Of course we could live without the internet. But we don't want to. This is a life-enhancing expense so we won't try to save money on it. Once again, don't deprive yourself.

Taxes on the other hand don't add any enjoyment to my life. I pay whatever I have to because that's the law and also the price you pay for being a member of a stable society. Regardless of the amount I *personally* pay in taxes, the level of service I receive from the various levels of government will not change. There are no special hospitals, schools, or libraries for people who pay more in taxes. Everyone gets the same level of service regardless of the amount of taxes they individually pay. That's why some people spend lots of money hiring attorneys and accountants to minimize how much tax they pay. Taxes are usually your biggest non life-enhancing expense so that's why we will cover ways to save on taxes later in the book.

Here's a real life example to help illustrate this concept. An acquaintance I knew while living in Ottawa was in the habit of making withdrawals from any bank's ATM machine. One time I mentioned that the bank machines that did not belong to her own bank probably charged her more than a $1 each time she used them. She shrugged and told me that she averaged about $30 a month in ATM service charges.

I knew that her salary was only $25,000 per year, which worked out to about $500 per week *before expenses* (income taxes, Canada Pension Plan Premiums (CPP), Employment Insurance Premiums (EI), union dues, professional dues, transportation costs, etc.) or that she earned roughly $350 a week *after expenses*. A quick calculation tells me that if she spent $30 a month in service charges then she spent ($30 x 12) $360 a year on ATM fees. In other words, if she only changed how she withdrew her money from bank machines she could take one whole extra week of vacation every year and still have just as much money to spend on everything else! She was getting up and going to work for a whole week just for ATM charges.

Spending Idea #3:

> *Try to save as much as possible from non life-enhancing expenses.*

Paying anything more than you have to for non life-enhancing things is like heating your house in the middle of a January snow storm while leaving some windows open. This type of spending tends to become routine, but a quick analysis can lead you to change how you do things. Simply looking at your spending habits and making minor adjustments is like getting up and closing all those open windows where the heat is escaping. I'm not advocating turning the furnace off and wearing your winter clothes while freezing in your home. That would not be life-enhancing, that would be miserly. Small adjustments can do the trick and get you to retirement years sooner than you thought.

One final point to remember is that each dollar saved is an *after expense dollar* saved. If you had to work for it, you'd have to earn up to *two dollars* to replace it. This is because it is expensive to work for a living—income taxes, Canada Pension Plan premiums, Employment Insurance premiums, professional dues, union dues, transportation costs, etc. It's interesting to note that my friend above (the ATM example) would jump at the chance to work overtime shifts "because she could always use the extra money." However after all these extra expenses, she would only see a portion of the money she had worked for. This brings us to:

Spending Idea Number 4:

> *Saving money is twice as powerful as earning more money.*

You'll see a good example of this idea illustrated for you in the chapter "How Much Do You *Really* Need?" From your salary right now, calculate how much you actually have after all of your working expenses are paid? Remember to deduct all the costs from the amount you "gross" (earn before expenses). The net amount (final figure after expenses) might shock you. That's why the next chapter will focus on saving taxes.

15

THE TAX MAN COMETH, MY MONEY GOETH!

"The best things in life are free,
but sooner or later the government
will find a way to tax them."
Anonymous

You'd be surprised how many taxes you really pay if you sit down and think about it. If you are an employee, you pay almost 5% for CPP, 2.5% for E.I., a 16% federal income tax on your first $32,000, 23% above that, a 6% Ontario rate on the first $32,000, 9% above that...Then there are gas taxes, GST, PST, HST, property taxes, liquor taxes...

There's the old expression that nothing in this world is certain except death and taxes. The newer expression states that there's only one certainty in life—that you'll be taxed to death! Having mentioned all this, the idea of taxation in general is a good one.

If we as Canadians want to live in a society where there are numerous social programs, then taxation is necessary. We all like public health care, good schooling, paved roads, and other services. It is everyone's responsibility to pay his or her fair share of taxes. However, taking any allowable legal steps to reduce your tax bill will greatly enhance your chances of reaching retirement early. In fact, that is the right of every Canadian taxpayer and it is stated in the "Declaration of Taxpayer's Rights."

In many cases, taxes are a person's single biggest expense, even larger than housing costs. There are many ways in which you can reduce your tax bill. If you successfully reduce the taxes you pay, you can attain financial security a lot more quickly. This is of paramount importance if you want to retire as early as possible.

This chapter is meant to provide a basic overview of the personal income taxes we face. I am not a tax expert, although I do know certain keys points about our tax system. If you want a more in depth look at the Canadian income tax system or the Income Tax Act, I would recommend a book called, *Jacks on Tax*, written by Evelyn Jacks. In it you will find a thorough explanation of pretty much every facet of personal income taxes.

Taxes can be daunting to some and utterly boring to most, but a basic understanding of the tax system will enable you to consider all aspects whenever confronting a money decision and this could shave years off your working life (which will mean more years of retirement).

First off, if you look at a basic income tax form, you will find that there are four federal tax rates which are 16%, 22%, 26%, and 29%. On top of this you have three Provincial tax rates (in Ontario for example) of roughly 6%, 9%, and 11%. The Canadian tax system is called progressive because as you earn more money, not only does the total amount of taxes you pay go up, but the *rate of taxes* you pay also goes up. So income earned in the lower brackets is taxed at a lower rate.

In addition to the taxes listed above, income below certain thresholds also attract other deductions called CPP (Canada Pension Plan), at a rate of about 5%, and EI (Employment Insurance), at a rate of about 2.5%. These are deducted directly from your paycheck. For the sake of reaching the goal of retiring as early as possible, these deductions are also a form of taxation (you can't opt out here). So with the fact that CPP and EI are taken from employment earnings, we come to the first important tax fact:

Tax Fact #1:
Employment income is the highest taxed form of income

This is true. Whenever you work for money, you are paying a much higher rate of deductions than on other forms of income. In addition, there are other out of pocket expenses involved with working for a living. Think about what you pay for transportation, child care, dry cleaning, union dues, professional dues, lunches bought while you're in a hurry, and so on. Are these life-enhancing expenses? No. So your strategy should be to move to a situation where money works for you rather than you working for money as quickly as possible.

Interest earnings are one type of investment income and they are received through bank accounts, GICs (guaranteed investment certificates), bonds, money market accounts, etc. This brings us to the second important point about taxation.

Tax Fact #2: Interest income is the highest taxed investment income source.

That's right. If you earn interest income you will pay tax at your top rate, but you don't have to pay CPP or EI.

The next form of income is the earnings you get

from owning common shares in a company. There are two main ways you earn money from owning stocks. The first is the money you collect every year in the form of dividends (the company sends you a cheque every three months). The computation for dividends involves "grossing up" (tax jargon) your actual dividend payments by 25% and then paying tax on that greater amount. The grossing up of the dividend is offset by the Dividend Tax Credit you get. It's quite complicated and difficult to explain, so I've included an example illustration below:

You own 100 shares of Company X and it pays a dividend of $1 per share

Total dividends you received:	$100.00
Gross up (100 x 1.25 = 125)	
Amount of income you claim:	$125.00

So in this case, you would pay taxes on $125.00 at your top marginal rate. Suppose your income was low (you were in the lowest tax bracket). You'd calculate:

$125.00 x 22.05% (16% federal + 6.05% provincial) = $ 27.56

But you would also be eligible for the dividend tax credit. This tax credit works out to approximately

16.67% of the actual amount of dividends received (in our example, it would be $100.00) or 13.33% of the "grossed up" amount. Therefore, the federal dividend tax credit would be $16.67. The provincial tax credit in Ontario works out to approximately 38.5% of the federal rate (or approximately 5% of the "grossed up" amount), so that would work out to about a $6.42 tax credit. I know it's complicated, but don't fall asleep yet. The main gist of it is shown below.

You have:

The income tax (from above)	$ 27.65
The federal dividend tax credit (16.67% x $100)	–($16.67)
The Ontario dividend tax credit ($16.67 x 38.5%)	–($ 6.42)
Total Taxes you pay	**$ 4.56**

Once again, it's a very involved computation, but the final result (and we're using rough estimates here) would be:

Dividend Income	$ 100.00
Taxes ($27.56–$16.67–$6.42)	($ 4.56)
Total left in your pocket	**$ 95.44**

It requires a lot of calculations (now you understand why I didn't follow a career in accounting!), but just look at the chart below and you'll see the main point. These are the rates for working income, interest income and dividend income.

	Working	Interest	Dividend
Income	$100.00	$100.00	$100.00
CPP (@4.95%)	($ 4.95)	nil	nil
EI (@2.5%)	($ 2.50)	nil	nil
Taxes (rate 22.05%)	($ 22.05)	($ 22.05)	($ 4.46)
Total you keep:	**$ 70.50**	**$ 77.95**	**$ 95.54**

From the above chart you can see how advantageous it is to move from employment income to dividend income.

The other way you earn money by owning common stocks is in the form of capital gains. Here you earn money on the difference between what you paid for your shares and what you sell them for. This income is only taxed at half the rate of regular income. In other words, whatever your capital gain is (the money you earned), you simply multiply it by half and then use that reduced amount as income. Using the same tax rates as above, the following table will illustrate the point:

Amount of capital gain:	$100.00
Amount claimed as income: (100x 0.5 = $50)	$ 50.00
Taxes Payable: ($50 x 22.05%)	$ (11.03)
Total you keep	**$ 88.97**

This leads us to the third point about taxation.

Tax Fact #3: Income from dividends or capital gains attracts a much lower rate of tax than employment or interest income.

This is a very important fact! If you want to retire as early as possible, your goal should be to move away from working for money towards investing for money. It is here where you get to keep more of your earnings. I know that most people need to work to live, but if you gradually shift to earning money from investments you'll benefit from paying much lower tax rates.

The final point we'll mention is in the area of investment trusts. There is no set rule for these as the tax rates they pay depend on a myriad of factors. We won't go into the details because it's much too complicated. Just remember:

Tax Fact #4. Investment trust income usually attracts a low rate of tax.

There are two other strategies you can use to further reduce your tax bill. The first method is tax deferral. This is simply finding ways to pay your taxes later (in some cases, many years later) then you would normally have to. I'll use an example to show the effectiveness of this strategy.

Suppose back in 1970 Mr. and Mrs. Average owed $10,000 to the tax department. The tax department agrees (because of whatever tax laws apply) that Mr. and Mrs. Average don't have to pay the $10,000 right away, but can defer that payment. So the Averages go out and buy a very nice house with the $10,000 (things were much cheaper more than thirty years ago). So the years go by and they are able to delay paying the taxes they owe. Finally, in 2004, the Averages decide to sell their house and get something a little smaller out in the country (they're not working anymore). They sell their nice house for $300,000 and buy something a little smaller for $200,000. They pay the $10,000 tax bill and put the other $90,000 in the bank. They've earned $290,000 by simply deferring the taxes.

Tax Fact #5: Deferring taxes is a great way to accumulate wealth.

From this simple example it's easy to see how deferring taxes can be a powerful tool. But how can you do it? Canada Revenue Agency doesn't just let you defer taxes just because you want to. There are only specific legal ways in which you can do this. For example, an RRSP is a tax deferral mechanism. You get a tax rebate for your current contribution and you are taxed on the money only when you take it out. That's one of the main advantages they offer. We'll examine RRSPs more closely in another chapter.

The main method I use to defer taxes is when I buy investments such as stocks. By buying and never selling, you defer paying taxes. This is one of the reasons why I advocate "buy and hold investing." Once you've found a great investment, your goal should be to never sell it. You should just sit back and collect the dividends every year.

Here's an example to show you the power of this tax saving strategy. Suppose there are two brothers, A and B. Brother A finds an investment that gains 15% a year for 25 years. He invests $10,000 and never sells. Brother B also earns 15% a year, but each year he sells his investment, pays his taxes and buys another one that gains 15%. He also invests for 25 years. Here's what happens:

Brother A has approximately $329,000 after 25 years. He sells the investments and pays his tax of roughly $82,000 (25% capital gains rate) and is left with almost **$247,000.**

Brother B has already paid his tax (25% capital gains rate) each year, so he doesn't have a big tax bill to pay at the end. But his final total is only **$145,000.**

Both brothers earned the same rate (15%),

invested for the same amount of time (25 years), and paid the same tax rate (25% of gains), but the brother who was a "buy and hold" investor reaped over $100,000 more simply by not selling until the end! Deferring taxes is a key to paying less in taxes.

Special tip: "Lazy investors reap more profits than active investors!"

The final strategy for reducing tax involves what's called "income splitting." Here in Canada, we have what's known as a progressive tax system. That means that as your income rises, you pay higher rates of tax. So essentially, the lower your income, the lower the *rate* of tax you pay. Now suppose you have two different couples. With couple A, one spouse earns $60,000 a year and the other doesn't earn any income. They do not do any tax planning. Here's what their taxes would look like if they had no other deductions (for simplicity sake, this is a rough estimation based on Ontario taxes):

Couple A	
Income	$ 60,000
Personal Deduction (about $15,000 per couple)	nil
Taxes (income ($32,250 -$15,000) x 22.05%)	$ (3,804)
Taxes (income ($60,000–$32,250) x 31.15%)	$ (8,644)
Total Taxes Paid	**$(12,448)**

Couple B splits their income such that each of them earns $30,000. In this case, their tax rates would fall and the total amount of taxes they would have to pay would be reduced. Here's the calculation below:

Couple B		
Income	$30,000	$30,000
Personal deductions (about $7,800 each)	nil	nil
Taxes (income ($30,000-$7,800) x 22.05%)	$(4,895)	$ (4,895)
Total Taxes Paid ($4,895 x 2)		**$(9,790)**

As you can see, both couple A and B earned the same amount of money before tax. But since couple A didn't split their income, their total tax bill was almost $3,000 more than couple B, who split their income. What would you do with $3000 more each and every year? If you compound this rate over many years of retirement, it can add up to amazing sums.

Tax Fact #6: Split income with other family members wherever possible.

But how can you do this? If you are working for a living, there is not much you can do to achieve income splitting. If you are self-employed, you can hire your spouse or children to do some of the work you do to split your income and lower your tax bill. Make sure you follow the guidelines set out by the tax department before you go ahead with this strategy.

It's easier to split investment income. If you earn money and contribute to an RRSP, contribute to your spouse's RRSP as well. Therefore both of your incomes will be the same in retirement so that you'll minimize taxes. There is more about this in the RRSP chapter.

If you receive the Child Tax Credit, have the money go to the spouse with the lower income. Then if that lower income spouse invests the money, the earnings from the investments are taxed in his/her hands and hence, pay a lower rate of tax. You could also have an official loan arranged whereby the higher income spouse lends money to the lower income spouse. The money could be used to buy investments. The investment income in this case would also be taxed in the hands of the lower income spouse. Just make sure you follow all the rules set out by the Canada Revenue Agency. The whole process may seem complex, but once you make a few simple adjustments, you could save thousands of dollars every year. In the above example, if the second couple had a little over thirty years of retirement (which is definitely possible), they would save almost $100,000 in taxes!

This chapter is not meant to provide you with a comprehensive look at the Canadian Income Tax Act. The examples and calculations are not precise.

Rather, they are used for illustrative purposes only. Income Tax is an extremely complicated subject. If you don't understand all of the above, that's okay. Simply remember the following key points:

1. If you work for money, you'll end up paying a lot more tax then if you have your money work for you!
2. Defer taxes whenever you can ($1 today is worth more than $1 tomorrow).
3. Splitting income with family members will reduce your total tax bill.

16

HOME IS WHERE THEY SEND MY BILLS

"If the real estate gang could,
they'd raise the rents in the graveyard"

Frank Dane

What is the single biggest purchase the average couple will ever make?

Many people say that their biggest investment is their home. This is understandable, as everyone needs to live somewhere and a house is generally the largest tangible purchase most people ever make. But the correct answer to the question above is actually the mortgage. Now some people could argue that a mortgage is not actually a "purchase." Fair enough but the main point is that in the grand scheme of things a mortgage is a huge financial decision. In many cases a mortgage will cost you more than *twice as much money* as the initial home purchase price.

If you've ever bought a resale home (a home being sold by an individual rather than a builder) then you know the tremendous amount of negotiating that can occur. I remember my wife and I once made an offer on a home and the deal was being negotiated throughout the night. Towards the end we were bargaining for a couple of used appliances and a floor mat! The point of mentioning this is to illustrate how seriously people look to try to get the best deal possible on a house.

It's surprising the number of people who will look for months to find the perfect house, then negotiate relentlessly to get the best possible deal on it and then just pay whatever the posted mortgage rate happens to be at their bank. This sort of action is like stepping over dollar bills to pick up pennies! This brings us to the first rule:

Housing Tip #1: Never pay the posted mortgage rates at your bank. Negotiate!

In addition, get several quotes before choosing a mortgage. There are some financial institutions out there like internet banks or insurance companies that really want your mortgage business so shop around. Also negotiate the fees. Sometimes banks will charge appraisal fees for the mortgage, but they may waive these fees if you ask. When my wife and I bought our house a few years ago, we asked the bank to waive the appraisal fee and it was no problem. You can also call a few lawyers and go with the cheapest one. We saved $300 by making four phone calls before choosing our lawyer. Searching title doesn't require the highest priced lawyer in the city.

Hint: Look for the lawyers with the smallest ads in the phone book.

If you want to save more money, avoid the CMHC fees by putting 25% of the purchase price down. This can be difficult for many people but it can save you a lot if you're in the position to do so. If you only put the minimum down and borrow the rest, your CMHC fees will be almost 4% of the purchase price. On an average home, that would be more than $5,000. Even if you're able to come up with at least a 10% down payment, the fees drop to 2.5%, which would save you thousands of dollars.

When purchasing a house most people feel a range of emotions from euphoria to anxiety. They are so focused on the actual transaction itself that they often neglect to think about all the fees they are asked to pay. This is because these extra charges seem so trivial when compared to the actual purchase price of the home and the mortgage. Just remember, a thousand here and a thousand there, and pretty soon you're talking some serious money!

Housing Tip #2: Try to save as much as possible on the fees levied when buying a house.

Once you've minimized the fees you have to pay, you should examine the mortgage and try to see what sort of prepayment options your mortgage offers. Some let you pay 20% of your original balance without any fees or extra charges while others aren't so generous. See if you can pay bi-weekly. This has the effect of making one extra payment a year and can get your mortgage paid off years earlier. There are so many options out there that we can't go over all of them. In sum, do whatever you can to eliminate your mortgage as quickly as possible. Paying off a mortgage is one of the best risk-free investments you can make.

Housing Tip #3: Paying off your mortgage is one of the best investments you can make.

Over the last few years interest rates have come down substantially. This has encouraged many people to buy bigger houses than they really need. Houses are so affordable right now because interest rates are so low. However, this is a sort of mirage. Over the life of your mortgage it might not be cheaper to make your payments then it was years ago. Let me explain.

The main reason why interest rates have come down so much is that inflation is not as high as it used to be. This means that although your initial payments will be lower than they would have been many years ago, you won't get help from inflation to reduce your housing costs as a percentage of your income over time. Years ago inflation would keep increasing your salary while the mortgage costs would remain fixed, so that over time the burden of carrying the mortgage would be a lower percentage of your salary. Now that inflation is low, your salary is not moving up as quickly as it used to. So don't listen to the old conventional "wisdom." If you do, you'll get stuck carrying a house that is really too expensive for you. You won't have any disposable income for anything else.

Nevertheless, owning a house is a very solid foundation in building a retirement. I love stocks and I love the stock market, but unfortunately stocks do not keep you warm in the winter or keep you from getting wet when it rains. Many investment professionals argue that one should rent a place and then invest the difference (as renting is generally cheaper in the short term). Under this scenario, the person should wind up with far more money over time. I flatly disagree.

First, we don't know how the stock market is going to do over the next year, five years, or ten years. Whenever you look at ads for various mutual funds, you always see seemingly impressive returns at the top of the ad in big block printing. It's only down near the bottom of the ad where you see the phrase, *"Past results are no guarantee of future returns."* It's always tempting to ignore this and focus on those nice big numbers up at the top of the ad. You take out your calculator (or use one of the online ones), and plug in a few numbers, and see in how short a time you can have $1 million or some other amount. The only trouble is that looking at those big numbers can be very misleading. Nobody can predict how the stock market is going to perform

An investment that can help you retire is something that puts money in your hands on a regular basis. Many people talk about how their houses have increased in value and this may be the case, but houses are NOT going to continue to increase like they've done in the past. The first few years of the millennium are not indicative of the norm. Buying a house is still a great investment if you plan on staying in one place for a while. There are a few reasons.

First, even though a house may cost more money every month in the beginning, over time mortgage payments remain more or less fixed (depending on interest rates), whereas rental amounts tend to increase over time. Eventually your housing costs for home ownership fall below the cost of renting.

Second, paying off a mortgage is a forced savings plan. Every month you can think that you own one more brick, another square foot, or another stair. Eventually, the whole place is yours and your living costs by then are much lower than if you had rented.

Housing Tip #4: Focus on home-ownership as a means to lower your living costs.

People don't get scared out of houses. It was shocking to look at mutual fund money flows during the 2000-2002 bear market. People were redeeming their stock mutual funds after they had already taken a beating. They had decided to run for cover and get out regardless of the costs. This fear is understandable. We had headlines of how Enron had collapsed and story after story of faulty accounting. It was hard to know what to believe. Many investors lost a lot of money. But every morning, you knew your house was still standing. You could touch it, feel it, and live in it. If housing prices fall, people don't panic. It still keeps the rain off your head and keeps you warm in the winter.

In addition, houses tend to be a pretty good hedge against inflation. Generally housing prices go up a little faster than the rate of inflation. This is because the people paid to build the houses are right here in North America. You can't outsource plumbing, wiring, or construction.

Manufactured goods have fallen in price over time as they've been made in low cost countries. If you wanted to buy a T.V. in the late 1970's, it would have cost you a small fortune. It was a sizeable purchase.

These days unless you're buying a special TV(flat screen, etc.), you can purchase one at a reasonable price. In the early 1980's people used to pay to get their TVs fixed. Now it's more economical to just throw it out and buy a new one. This is because the people paid to make TVs are living in low wage countries and earn a small fraction of what the average North American earns. If you pay someone to fix your TV, you're paying North American wage rates, so they're often too expensive to fix. This is the case with housing. All the labour must be done by people earning North American wage rates so this helps prices keep up with inflation.

To reiterate, houses put money in your pocket by reducing your housing costs in the long run. Buying a house should be an early step in your plan to retire. The next chapter will deal with limiting or eliminating debt.

17

I OWE. I OWE. THERE'S LOTS OF WORK TO GO!

"Neither a borrower nor a lender be"

William Shakespeare

Previous generations took the above advice to heart. These are the words many parents would say to their children as they were about to enter the wide world on their own. People would try to avoid debt at all costs. If they did incur some, they would try to pay it off as quickly as possible. Debt was viewed as a burden. Why is this?

Many people from earlier generations came to North America through debt. They came here as indentured servants. Immigrants chose this option because life in Europe was so bleak and hopeless. So they toiled day in and day out for years dreaming of the day their debts would be totally repaid.

Today debt is the norm for most people. In fact if you have no debt you are truly in the minority. Most people have incurred debt for a variety of reasons. Mortgage debt is the most common but there are so many other forms of debt. People buy cars on credit or lease them, which is also an indirect form of debt. Students fund their university education by racking up enormous debts in many cases. People also celebrate Christmas by using their credit cards to buy their family members numerous presents and then spend the New Year trying to pay it all off. Simply put, debt has become a way of life.

In a nutshell, debt is the biggest obstacle to retirement for most people. It's a sort of Pandora's Box inviting you to spend a little of your future hard earned money. It has many allies in its quest to separate you from your money. People are continually bombarded with T.V commercials, advertisements, and the like sending a message that if you just bought this or that gadget, your life would be remarkably improved. It's so easy to take out a credit card and hand it to the store clerk and walk out with whatever item you desire. The difficult part comes later, when you have to try to pay all those cards off.

The number of bankruptcies has been rising over the last couple of decades. Money and debt is one of the leading causes of divorce. At a minimum, debt can keep you working at a job you really don't like for many years longer than you want and delay or prevent you from retiring and achieving your dreams.

I remember this idea being explained with a simple bumper sticker. It was a play on words of a song in the movie "Snow White." It stated simply, "I owe, I owe, so it's off to work I go." I never thought I'd get financial advice from a bumper sticker, but there you have it.

Let's examine the various forms of debt and see how they affect your financial security over time. Here are the main ones.

1. Credit Card Debt

It's a fact of life that you would be severely restricted without having a credit card. If you want to rent a car, order something over the internet, reserve a hotel room, and a host of other things, you need a credit card. There are numerous cards that give you anything from points towards a new car, to groceries, to air miles, to many other "freebies."

Credit card businesses can afford these because they charge very high rates of interest—higher than 20% in some instances! Essentially, consumer credit card debt is the absolute worst sort of debt to have. If you use credit cards, pay the entire balance off every month. This brings us to debt rule number one:

Debt Rule #1: If you have a credit card, never carry a balance.

As appealing as consumer debt is in the short term, (don't pay anything now but enjoy the item right away), if used too much it can have serious consequences. These results can range from situations where you run faster and faster on the working treadmill but don't get to enjoy the fruits of your labour as you are too busy paying off interest, to outright bankruptcy for serious cases. Debt is a ball and chain preventing you from achieving financial security and the freedom to choose your own destiny. Getting out of debt and staying out of debt is the most important thing you can do to reach early retirement.

2. Car Loans and Leases

It is easier to avoid credit card debt than to avoid car loans. To drive a new car, most people need to get a car loan or lease the car. This form of debt is not nearly as bad a credit card debt because the rates are usually a lot lower. However, there are a few ways you can reduce or avoid this expense.

Here's one way I found. A while ago I put a little extra money away every month. By doing this over time, I created a sizeable lump sum. I use this money whenever I want to buy a new car and then I continue to make car payments, but I make them to my "car account."

Debt Rule #2: Pay cash for your car and then make the payments (to yourself!)

A variation on this is to make investments that can buy your car for you. This strategy would work best if you already had a paid off house. Here's how it works.

First get a secured line of credit on your house for around $65,000. You can easily get one of these at prime (a very low interest rate). The interest rate at time of writing is 4%.

Next, take this money and buy 1000 shares of Corby Distilleries (at $65 each). Corby is just one example, but you probably should spread your money over a number of investments. I'm just using one stock here for simplicity sake.

Corby was covered earlier but to summarize, it produces liquor and is a stable company which pays a $2.20/share dividend every year. In addition it also pays an enormous $16.50 special dividend every five years or so. If you purchased 1000 shares, you would receive $2,200 every year and a special dividend of $16,500 every five years or so.

The strategy is to drive your existing car until Corby pays the special dividend. Then take the $16,500 cheque to the car dealership. Trade in your old car, add the $16,500 from the special dividend, and get a brand new car—without any payments! This is one case where combining alcohol and cars would be okay but not at the same time!

But what about the interest on your loan? How would you pay this?

Your interest costs would amount to ($65,000 x 4%) $2,600 per year in interest. But since the money you borrowed was used to buy stocks and earn income, the interest would be *tax deductible*. In this case, you would save anywhere from $600 to over $1,200 a year in taxes. So your actual costs would be $1,400—$2,000 (interest cost *less* tax savings) a year.

Debt Rule #3: Tax-deductible debt is the best kind of debt to have.

Remember, Corby would be paying you a regular dividend of ($2.20 per share x 1000 shares) $2,200 a year. Also remember that dividends are taxed at a low rate (from the tax chapter). So you could use the regular dividends to pay the interest on your loan and the special dividends would pay for your new car every few years. The whole process would cost you nothing! It would be like having a "company car," provided to you by Corby Distilleries.

The risk of this strategy is if interest rates rise substantially. This risk can be offset by waiting for the perfect time to buy Corby stock. Wait for the "buttonless elevator" known as the stock market to begin falling then buy the shares. In 2001 Corby traded for as low as $45 a share. In this case, your regular dividend would become ($2.20 divided by $45) almost 5%. But the amount you borrow would only be $45,000 instead of $65,000. This would decrease your interest costs and lower your risk. Remember, patience is the key.

3. Student Debt

Student debt has become a reality for young people in Canada these days. Over the last number of years, governments have cut back funding for post-secondary education. As a result, tuition costs have soared. Making matters worse is the fact that many students who graduate cannot find high enough paying jobs to make the payments on these enormous loans. As my cousin puts it, "You end up having a mortgage without the house to go along with it."

What can students do? First, don't feel pressured to rush head long into university just because that seems like the next logical step. I'm not saying don't go to university. I hope both of my children eventually get a degree. I'm just saying that people should make sure they know what they want to study before starting.

Once you've decided what you want to study, try to find whatever free money is available. There are many grants offered that never have to be paid back, especially for good students. Check to see what's available on the internet.

Debt Rule #4: If you're a student, minimize the amount of debt you take on.

In addition, you should try to have a part time job to help defray the costs somewhat and limit the amount of debt you need.

Finally for parents, if you have extra money and want to save up for your child(ren)'s education, there are various ways to do it. Check out RESPs (Registered Education Saving Plans) where income you earn in the account grows tax free and the government contributes some additional money (20% of what you contribute). You can invest in GICs, mutual funds, or have a self-directed plan where you can hold stocks. There are many considerations regarding what to invest in and you should do your research before deciding.

The main disadvantage to RESPs is that you have to cash out your investments at a certain time—when your child goes to university. So when you are within ten years or so of needing the money, gradually convert the equity portion (stocks) into interest bearing investments (bonds, GICs, etc.). This will protect you if the stock markets start to fall. I know that I already said that I love stocks but in this case you must cash out the plan at a specified time, so you can't merely collect your dividends forever—that's the weakness of these plans. My investment strategy doesn't work if you must take your money out at a certain time. You *are* dependent on the ups and downs of the stock market, so that's why I advocate buying bonds or GICs within ten years of needing the money—safety first!

Also remember that any money you get from the Child Tax Credit can be invested in the name of your child and this income is taxed in the hands of your child (which often means no tax at all). Check with the Canadian Revenue Agency for all the rules relating to this.

In summation, avoid non-deductible debt whenever possible but also look to tax deductible investment debt as a means to help you achieve your goals. The next chapter will look at the most commonly advertised tax deferral vehicle in Canada—the RRSP.

18

RRSPS? NO THANK YOU

"I am opposed to millionaires,
but it would be dangerous to offer me the position."
Mark Twain

If you read about investing, you will invariably come across information relating to RRSPs. The first thing you need to know is, "What exactly is an RRSP?"

An RRSP is a Registered Retirement Savings Plan. It is NOT an investment in and of itself. In other words it's not similar to stocks, bonds, money market accounts, and things like that. An RRSP is merely a separate account where you can hold various investments that are subject to a different set of tax rules. Within an RRSP you can hold a variety of investments like stocks, bonds, mutual funds, etc. Just like many people have separate accounts like savings and chequing accounts, they can also have another account called an RRSP account.

We are constantly being bombarded with information about RRSPs. In a sense they have become another event each calendar year. Just like the countdown before each and every Christmas, "Only 12 shopping days left!" a lot is also made of the RRSP deadline of March first every year. March 1 is usually the last day of the year you can make your contribution for the previous year's return. If you miss the deadline, your contribution will affect your subsequent year's taxes.

Too much is made of this deadline. Have you ever thought about that word? What a scary term—"dead-line."

The other main point you will see mentioned is how many Canadians simply aren't "maxing out" their RRSP contributions. This simply means that they are not contributing their absolute maximum amounts every year. This fact is sort of presented in such a way that if you haven't maxed out your contribution this year, you have failed in this area. You might suffer dire financial consequences down the road—cat food for dinner and a cardboard box under a bridge somewhere as your home when you retire if you don't contribute the maximum!

What is the maximum anyway? It is 18% of your previous year's earned income up to a maximum of $15,500 in 2004, $16,500 in 2005, and $18,000 in 2006.

That's the basic overview of RRSPs. Now why do people contribute to them? Basically, for every dollar you contribute, your income is considered to be reduced by a dollar in the eyes of the federal and provincial governments that charge you income tax. So you will get some immediate tax savings. In addition, once the money is in this separate account, it can grow tax-free for years until you want to take it out. When you finally do take it out, you would have to pay taxes on it. This is the reason it is often seen as a good way to save for retirement.

Should you contribute to RRSPs? This is one of the trickiest questions in planning for retirement. If you have a low enough income (below $32,000), then I would say NOT to contribute to your RRSP. This is because the immediate tax savings you get will be lower than if you were a higher income earner.

RRSP Tip #1: It may be better not to contribute if your income is below $32,000.

Now there are exceptions to this. If you are going to take a year off work in the next few years you may want to contribute this year and get the tax savings. Then you might avoid the tax on withdrawals altogether if your income is low enough the year you take off.

What if your income is a lot higher and you are in a higher tax bracket? Should you contribute then? This is really where the water gets muddy and there is no absolute clear winner here. I personally like the idea of paying off your mortgage as quickly as possible. Although you are using after tax dollars to make the mortgage payments, once your mortgage is fully paid off, you are saving after tax dollars in expenses.

Some experts argue that if you delay contributing to your RRSP, then you lose the benefit of tax-free compounding which could amount to hundreds of thousands of dollars. This could be true if the markets perform very well. But what if we get a stock market like the one from 1964–1981in the U.S. where it essentially did not go up for 17 years?

One point I'd like to add is that you should also look at your own personality. Money decisions are not only financial in nature. I know this statement might sound strange at first, but it's very important. If you are the type of person who is going to look at your RRSP account balance every month and lose sleep if the balance has taken a hit due to a stock market meltdown (the first few years of the new millennium would have been a good test), then you should just focus on paying off your mortgage first. It's very difficult to put a price on peace of mind. Eliminating a mortgage is not a bad financial option either.

RRSP Tip #2: Although contributing to your RRSP can be a great move, so is paying off your mortgage early.

Here's another possibility. Suppose you earn a high income right now but you expect your income to continue to increase. An RRSP strategy might not be your best option. Instead you could focus on paying off your mortgage as quickly as possible. Then once it is completely paid off, you could get a loan secured by the equity of your house. Use this money to buy investments outside of your RRSP. This way you are going to get a tax deduction on all the interest you pay for the duration of the loan. If you buy stocks that pay consistent dividends, you'll be getting tax advantages because dividend income is lightly taxed. In contrast, money taken from an RRSP pays tax at your top marginal rate!

RRSP Tip #3: Borrowing money from a paid off home and investing it can be a better strategy than buying RRSPs.

From the information I've provided about RRSPs you can probably guess that I am not a huge fan of them personally. This is because you must start cashing out your investments at a certain time—once you reach 69. Unless you only buy interest bearing investments (bonds, GICs, etc.), you *are* dependent on the ups and downs of the stock market.

However, there is one area where an RRSP is a phenomenal tool that can accelerate your trip to retirement. This is in the area of income splitting. I explained the benefits of income splitting in detail in the taxation chapter. An RRSP is a great tool to split income.

If one spouse earns substantially more than the other, have the high income spouse contribute to a spousal RRSP. In this case you will still get the regular tax deduction, but the money will have been transferred into your spouse's name. This does not have an immediate effect but when it comes time to retire, your income will be divided between the two of you so the total amount of taxes you have to pay will be much lower. This can also affect other expenses like the new Ontario Health Premium which increases with income levels. One special fact to remember is that the spouse receiving the contribution must keep the money in his/her RRSP for at least three years or else the money will be taxed in the hands of the spouse who originally made the contribution. Such planning can also make sense if one of the spouses is planning to stop working in order to have children. Make sure you follow the guidelines set out by the Canada Revenue Agency.

RRSP Tip #4: RRSPs can be used to split income between spouses to lower the overall taxes a family has to pay.

The main point of this chapter is to show that although RRSPs can be a good way to minimize taxes, they are not your only option. Consider paying off your mortgage more quickly or investing outside your RRSP. And remember, even if you're not "maxing out" your RRSP every year, you don't have to believe the hype that you are destined for a terrible retirement. I didn't focus on maxing out my RRSP. In fact I don't even have an RRSP, but I still managed to retire by 34.

19

HOW MUCH DO YOU REALLY **NEED?**

"Too little money makes people desperate; too much money makes people greedy."
Aristotle

In order to have a comfortable retirement, one in which you can do what you want without worrying about running out of money, you must figure out how much you really need. Now in the investment community there are a lot of figures batted around. Maybe you've heard you need 70% of pre-retirement income in order to maintain your lifestyle after retirement. Another estimate suggests a minimum nest egg of a million dollars to make sure you live comfortably. Whether or not you need this much depends on exactly what kind of retirement you plan on having. I don't have anywhere near $1 million. I don't earn 70% of the pre-tax median Canadian income. I am definitely not rich. Regardless of this, I live a very comfortable life!

Essentially the financial services industry increases profits by selling more financial products. These can include mutual funds, GICs, bonds, stocks, IPO's, life insurance, and a range of other products. In many instances you'll be encouraged to save as much as possible for as long as possible regardless of your actual need.

My own approach was different. My goal was to retire by the age of 35 and I achieved it one year early. My goal was not to save as much money as possible, but to save enough to live comfortably while having time to pursue my dreams

Before thinking about retiring you have to sit down and decide what it is you really want. What sort of lifestyle do *you* want? Then you need to figure out exactly how much it is going to cost you every year. Only then can you truly find the correct answer to how much you really need to retire.

Let's look at this by way of an old story. A few years ago, a very rich American businessman decides to take a vacation to a small tropical island in the South Pacific. He has worked hard all his life and has decided that now is the time to enjoy the fruits of his labour. He's excited about going to the island because he's heard there's incredible fishing there. He loved fishing as a young boy, but hasn't gone in years because he has been busy working to prepare for his retirement.

So the first day there, he has his breakfast and heads

down to the beach. It's around 10am. There he spots a fisherman coming in with a large bucket—full of fish!

"How long did you fish for?" he asks.

The fisherman looks at the rich businessman with a wide grin across his face and explains that he fishes for about three hours every day. The businessman then asks him why he returned so quickly. He's worried that all the fish are gone.

"Don't worry," says the fisherman, "There's still plenty of fish out there."

Dumbfounded, the businessman asks the fisherman why he didn't continue catching more fish. The fisherman patiently explains that what he caught is all he needs.

"I will spend the rest of the day playing with my family, talking with my friends, and maybe drinking a little wine. After that I'll relax on the beach."

Now the rich businessman figures he needs to teach this peasant fisherman a thing or two. So he explains to him that he should stay out all day and catch more fish. Then he could save up the extra money he makes and buy an even bigger boat to catch even more fish. Then he could keep reinvesting his profits in even more boats and hire many other fishermen to work for him. If he works very hard, in 20 or 30 years he'll be a very rich man indeed.

The businessman feels pleased that he's helped teach this simple fellow how to become rich. Then the fisherman looks at the businessman with a puzzled expression on his face and asks what he'll do after he becomes very rich.

The businessman responds quickly, "you can spend time with your family, talk with your friends, and maybe drink a little wine. Or you could just relax on the beach."

In the above example it's clear that the fisherman did not have to worry about saving up $1 million dollars or anything close to that to retire. His life was simple and he was happy. The story is very simplistic, but it shows that you don't necessarily need an enormous sum to retire. And it illustrates that you should figure out how much you'll need by yourself and not rely too heavily on the advice of others.

While calculating how to retire as quickly as possible I had to figure out how much money I would need. I've heard many people say things like, "Money's not important." or, "I don't care about money." Well I don't require a lot of things to be happy but I think money is very important. If you've ever been in the position of not having enough, you know the anxiety it can cause. Life is much better if you have enough money to make yourself comfortable and pursue your dreams. Or in the words of Mae West, "I've been rich and I've been poor, and rich is better."

Having said this, the total amount of money you require can be much lower than you think. Here's a formula you can use to calculate how much you really need to retire:

Total current income (your salary)

- (Work related expenses) (Taxes, EI, CPP, professional dues, etc.)
- (All interest expenses) (eliminate all debt before retirement)

\+ New lower tax expenses (Taxes on investment income)

\+ Costs for new hobbies (that's the reason you're retiring)

= **Total amount of income you'll need (after taxes)**

This can give you a figure for exactly how much you will need in your retirement. By paying off your debt you've reduced the amount of income you need. By shifting your earnings from working earnings to passive earnings, you've eliminated your work related expenses and reduced you total tax expenses. You add back any expenses you might incur for new interests or hobbies because your retirement should be a long enjoyable time. It is not a time to deprive yourself.

Here is a hypothetical example to give you an idea. Suppose you are the only salary earner in your family earning $60,000 a year working. Most families have two income earners these days, but for the sake of keeping the calculations simple, we'll use just one. Let's assume you're married with two children. You have a mortgaged house, car payments, but no other debt. You don't have a company pension plan and don't know exactly how much you will need to retire.

How much do you need to earn to maintain your current lifestyle?

Salary		$ 60,000
CPP costs	(minus)	$ (1,831)
EI costs	(minus)	$ (975)
Federal Tax (Taxes-Credits)	(minus)	$ (8,868)
Provincial Tax (Ontario)	(minus)	$ (3,569)
Provincial Health Premium	(minus)	$ (600)
Clothes (dry cleaning $10/week)	(minus)	$ (520)
Monthly bus pass ($80/month)	(minus)	$ (960)
Car payments ($300/month)	(minus)	$ (3,600)
Mortgage (175K @ 6.6% for 25yr.)	(minus)	$ (14,196)
Retirement Saving ($100 / month)	(minus)	$ (1,200)
Child Tax Credit (total 2 kids)	add	$ 1,416
GST Credit		nil
Total income (after expenses)		**$22,265**

You earn $22,265 after all your taxes and other work related expenses and savings are paid.

In the next chapter there's a sample portfolio provided that will give you an investment income of $18,845. This amount is less than one third what you would earn working (in the example above), but look at the final calculations:

Portfolio income		$ 18,845
CPP costs		nil
EI costs		nil
Federal Taxes		nil
Provincial Taxes		nil
Provincial Health Premium		nil
Clothes (dry cleaning)		nil
Monthly bus pass		nil
Car payments		nil
Mortgage		nil
Child Tax Credit (2 kids, add NCBS)	add	$ 5,222
GST Credit	add	$ 684
Total Income (after expenses)		**$ 24,751**

You don't pay CPP or EI because you are not working now. You don't pay any taxes because a lot of the securities in your portfolio provide you with tax-deferred income. Your income is also low enough that you no longer have to pay the Ontario Health Premium. In order to retire, you should get completely out of debt so that would eliminate the need for car and mortgage payments. You don't need to save for retirement because you're already retired. You would also get more money for GST and Child Tax Credits because your income is now lower. So how would you get to this stage?

A big hurdle is the mortgage. How much did you originally pay for your house? What's it worth now?

Any capital gains on your house when you sell it are tax free because it's your principle residence. Could you sell it and buy a smaller house? If you didn't have to work would you need to be living where you are now or could you move further out of the city and save money?

After people retire, it is common for them to sell their house that is close to their job and move into something either smaller or a little further from the big city. This usually puts a lot of extra money in their pocket because their existing house is much more expensive than the house they choose after they retire.

My personal example is a good one. I recently bought an average house a little over an hour away from Toronto. If I had to work in Toronto, I would have probably bought a house that was much closer to the city....and much more expensive! But the smaller town I'm living in now is much better for raising a family. There's more fresh air and open spaces. It has a "sense of community." So because I don't have to go into work every day, I was able to save money on my housing while also improving the quality of life my family now enjoys.

How much you'll need depends on the lifestyle you want. But don't blindly follow the standard formulas usually given. Figure out how much you *really* need. The next chapter will show you an example portfolio that can provide you with the income shown in the example above.

20

AN EXAMPLE PORTFOLIO

"The first man gets the oyster;
the second man gets the shell."

Andrew Carnegie

Below is a sample portfolio that should weather economic storms and provide a stable but growing income.

Investment	**# of Shares**	**Dividends/ share**	**Annual Income**
Riocan REIT	2500	$1.20	$3,000
Algonquin Power Fund	2500	$0.92	$2,300
Pembina Pipelines	2500	$1.05	$2,625
Pengrowth Trust	2500	$2.52	$6,300
Royal Bank (RBC Financial)	1000	$2.08	$2,080
George Weston Limited	1000	$1.44	$1,440
IGM Financial	1000	$1.10	$ 1,100
Total Income			**$18,845**

The above portfolio is merely a sample portfolio. This portfolio contains a mix of "show me the money now" investments balanced with some growth investments that should raise their dividends over time to offset the impact of future inflation. In practice it would be wiser to include more securities in your portfolio to achieve greater diversification but the above is good for explanation purposes. I am not advocating that you copy this portfolio as it's only meant as an example.

How much would this portfolio cost to assemble? Below is a list of the prices of the various securities at this time and a total cost calculation.

Investment	# of shares	Cost per share	Total Cost
Riocan	2500	$16.00	$ 40,000
Algonquin Power Fund	2500	$10.00	$ 25,000
Pembina Pipelines	2500	$ 11.30	$ 28,250
Pen Growth Trust	2500	$18.50	$ 46,250
Royal Bank (RBF)	1000	$61.00	$ 61,000
George Weston Limited	1000	$92.00	$ 92,000
IGM Financial	1000	$33.00	$ 33,000
Total Cost			**$325,500**

Now that's not nearly the $1 million dollars that is often mentioned as a bare minimum to avoid the dire fate of eating cat food to stay alive in retirement. But it's still a pretty sizeable amount. But of course, you usually don't construct a portfolio at once. You build it gradually over time. Time is your ally. Time allows you to watch that good old volatile stock market. When I was in Australia, I learned that crocodiles are ambush hunters who often wait hours for their prey to come to them and then they grab them. Think of the stock market as a hunting game, and wait for the "chicken littles" to run around and start to shout "the sky is falling." When this happens, whether it is happening in the whole market or to one individual stock, you pounce. Let's look at the above investments patiently acquired over time at better prices (*this is a real life example*):

Investment	**Date**	**# of shares**	**Cost per share**	**Total Cost**
Riocan	2000	2500	$ 8.00	$ 20,000
Algonquin Power	2000	2500	$ 7.00	$ 17,500
Pembina Pipelines	2000	2500	$ 7.00	$ 17,500
Pengrowth	1992	2500	$ 5.00	$ 12,500
Royal Bank	1996	1000	$ 15.00	$ 15,000
George Weston	1993	1000	$ 13.00	$ 13,000
IGM Financial	1995	1000	$ 8.00	$ 8,000
Total Cost				**$103,500**

As you can see, it is of the utmost importance not only to buy good investments but to buy them when everyone else is selling them. It is interesting to note that three of the investments (Riocan, Pembina, and Algonquin), could have all been bought around the same time the overall markets were hitting new highs with the technology stock bubble. At this time people were paying outrageous prices for technology stocks (many of which had never earned a profit), while ignoring some sound higher yielding investments like these.

There are two main points to remember. First, it does not take millions of dollars to create a comfortable retirement. How much you need depends on the lifestyle you want and how long you would like to postpone retirement. Second, by waiting patiently for the markets to give you good opportunities to buy (when most others are selling), you can really reduce the amount of money you need to save. This can allow you to retire years earlier than you thought.

21

YOUR JOURNEY BEGINS

"Even if you're on the right track, you'll get run over if you just sit there."
Will Rogers

The beginning of this book stated that the goal was to help you retire as early as possible without being held captive to the stock market. I mentioned that if you followed the ideas outlined, that you too could obtain freedom from the work world. Well you've almost made it to the end of the book. There are no more tips or suggestions to help you reach your goals and have the time to realize your dreams. The ball now moves into your court. What do you do from here?

There's a final story about a salesman that I heard long ago. Selling is a hard way to make a living and you have to be prepared for rejection all the time. So one fellow figured he'd become the perfect salesman. He went to the best hair stylist in town to do his hair.

He bought a perfect suit chosen with the help of image consultants to make sure he would be sending the perfect signal to prospective clients. He stood in front of the mirror day after day rehearsing exactly what to say, ensuring that he was using the correct intonation and his body language was congruent with his words. He felt he was almost ready when he got a phone call from head office. He was fired! He never actually got around to just doing it.

Don't be like this salesman. Don't put this book up on the shelf and forget about it.

There's a saying that small actions, however insignificant, are infinitely more powerful than even the grandest of intentions. Take action! If you follow the advice in this book you *will* reach retirement sooner. Although my case is exceptional, this strategy is exactly what I did to retire by 34.

Start your journey today. Time is your most valuable asset. Pursue your dreams!

RECOMMENDED READING LIST

"Learning is a treasure that will follow its owner everywhere."

Chinese Proverb

The Wealthy Barber (financial planning)
David Chilton

One Up on Wall Street: How To Use What You Already Know To Make Money in the Market (investing)
Peter Lynch

Beating the Street (investing) Peter Lynch

The Warren Buffett Way: Investment Strategies of the World's Greatest Investor (investing)
Robert Hagstrom

Jacks on Tax (tax information) Evelyn Jacks

The Joy of Not Working (fulfillment in not working)
Ernie Zelinski

Common Stocks and Uncommon Profits (investing) Philip Fisher

The Intelligent Investor (investing) Ben Graham

(Annual Reports) Berkshire Hathaway (varied) Warren Buffett

The Money Masters: Nine Great Investors: Their Strategies and How You Can Apply Them (investing) John Train

* These books are simply suggested readings. Some of the information may be out of date. You should always seek professional advice related to tax, investment, financial, and legal issues before taking action on your own.